CREATIVE
WRITING
MAGIC

CREATIVE WRITING MAGIC

80 TIPS AND TRICKS FOR YOUNG WRITERS

ANDY JONES (WITH A LITTLE MORE HELP FROM RUBY & EVIE)

ILLUSTRATIONS BY Olaf Falafel

FOR MOUSE & ROOSTER. NOT SO LITTLE ANY MORE,
BUT ALWAYS MY MONSTERS XX
— A.J.

FOR ALL THE YOUNG AUTHOR, ILLUSTRATOR AND
COMEDIAN MONSTERS OUT THERE - ENJOY!
— O.F.

FIRST PUBLISHED 2026 BY WALKER BOOKS LTD, 87 VAUXHALL WALK, LONDON SE11 5HJ

2 4 6 8 10 9 7 5 3 1

EU AUTHORIZED REPRESENTATIVE: HACKETTFLYNN LTD, 36 CLOCH CHOIRNEAL, BALROTHERY, CO. DUBLIN, K32 C942, IRELAND. EU@WALKERPUBLISHINGGROUP.COM

THIS BOOK HAS BEEN TYPESET IN STEMPEL SCHNEIDLER, CHALKDUSTER, LIQUID EMBRACE AND HALEWYN

PRINTED IN CHINA

BRITISH LIBRARY CATALOGUING IN PUBLICATION DATA: A CATALOGUE RECORD FOR THIS BOOK IS AVAILABLE FROM THE BRITISH LIBRARY

ISBN 978-1-4063-9663-8

WWW.WALKER.CO.UK

CONTENTS

SECTION TWO: CREATING MAGICAL CHARACTERS

SECTION THREE: WHEN THE MAGIC ISN'T HAPPENING

SECTION FOUR: IN SEARCH OF MAGIC

FIRST, LET'S MEET **ANDY** WHO WROTE THIS BOOK

THREE YEARS AGO - OR WAS IT FOUR? - I WROTE *UNLEASH YOUR CREATIVE MONSTER*. I WROTE IT FOR MY DAUGHTERS - EVIE AND RUBY - AND TO INSPIRE ANY OTHER CHILDREN THAT WERE INTERESTED IN CREATIVE WRITING. BUT A FUNNY THING HAPPENED. BEFORE CREATIVE MONSTER, I HAD WRITTEN FIVE NOVELS FOR GROWN-UPS. BUT SINCE THEN, I HAVE WRITTEN THREE NOVELS FOR CHILDREN, WITH MORE TO COME (YOU SHOULD CHECK THEM OUT!). SO I GUESS I ENDED UP INSPIRING MYSELF! I HOPE THIS BOOK DOES THE SAME FOR YOU.

AND OLAF WHO DREW THE PICTURES

HI AGAIN, OLAF HERE! I'M STILL AN AUTHOR, AN ILLUSTRATOR, A DAD, AND YES, STILL A STAND-UP COMEDIAN – I KEEP TRYING BUT I STILL HAVEN'T MASTERED THE ART OF "CHANGING COLOURS LIKE A STAND-UP CHAMELEON"! THIS TIME ROUND I'VE CREATED EVEN MORE MONSTERS, COMPLETE WITH FUNNY THINGS COMING OUT OF THEIR MOUTHS. IF YOU WERE TO ASK WHAT MY FAVOURITE DRAWINGS IN THIS BOOK WERE, I'D PROBABLY SAY POOPY BIRD MONSTER ON PAGE 93 AND THE BOY WHO TRIES DESPERATELY HARD NOT TO MENTION HIS TEACHER'S WART ON PAGE 136 – THAT REALLY MADE ME LAUGH. THERE IS A SECTION ON PAGE 154–55 THAT SHOWS YOU SOME OF THE STUPID THINGS THAT LIVE IN MY HEAD, INCLUDING A FARTING HOT-AIR BALLOON. I HOPE THIS BOOK INSPIRES YOU TO CREATE MONSTERS, WRITE STORIES AND MAYBE EVEN START TELLING JOKES! WHO KNOWS, MAYBE ONE DAY YOU'LL BE A STAND-UP CHAMELEON!

THE CREATIVE MONSTER RETURNS

NOW WITH ADDED MAGIC!!!

Hello there! Welcome to the second Creative Monster book. Just like the first book, it's full of tips and tricks to help you add a little sparkle to your writing. You'll find dozens of story prompts, tons of monsters, some ideas for finding ideas, and – something new for this book – a sprinkling of creative projects for your Creative Monster to sink its teeth into.

Don't worry if you haven't read *Unleash Your Creative Monster* – all the ideas in this book are easy to understand. I say that with confidence because I live with two little monsters (my daughters Ruby and Evie), and before anything goes in this book, they read it to check it all makes sense. If it doesn't, they send me back to my office and don't let me out until I've got it right (they're very strict children!).

As you read this, I imagine you're thinking one of two things:

Thing One **(thought by people who read the first Creative Monster book):**

Thing Two **(thought by people who didn't):**

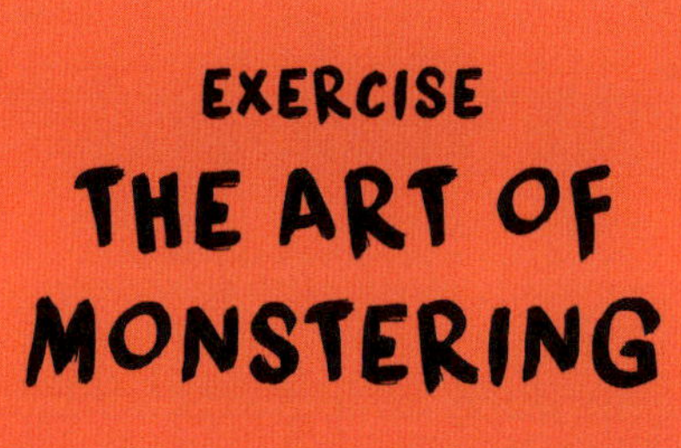

EXERCISE

THE ART OF MONSTERING

If you're new to Creative Monstering, why not draw your own Creative Monster now? Draw a monster that reflects your personality, the stories you enjoy reading, and those you would like to write.

If, on the other hand (or paw, claw, tentacle), you have read book one and are now an expert Monsterer, why not redraw your Creative Monster, showing how it has grown and developed.

MAGIC
TRICKS
FOR
WRITERS

LEVEL 1

SIMPLE SPELLS FOR SCRIBBLERS

So what's all this about magic?

Allow me to explain:

If you're anything like me, you'll love getting lost in a great story. But what is it that makes some stories affect us more than others? The answer is … MAGIC!

Stories amaze, mystify and delight. In short, they cast a spell over us.

This section contains a selection of simple tricks that you can use to add a little magic to your own stories. So, grab your pencil (the writer's magic wand) and disappear for a while in the following pages…

MAGICAL INGREDIENTS FOR ANY STORY

GOALS, OBSTACLES AND STRUGGLES

Just as a witch needs various bits and bobs (eye of newt, nose-hair of dragon, fart of monkey) to make potions and cast spells, writers need special ingredients to create their own magic – in other words to write stories. Those ingredients are: goals, obstacles and struggles.

The main character (or characters) in your story must have a *goal*. Something they desperately want to achieve or do. For example:

If this goal is easy, then the story is boring. So we must make it difficult for our characters by placing ***obstacles*** in their path. Things like an enemy, a broken leg, a treacherous mountain, an escaped gorilla or a hurricane. Even something as simple as a lack of confidence makes a great story obstacle.

Finally, your character must ***struggle*** – they must fight against the obstacles to achieve their goal. They must be brave, cunning, clever and determined. They must be a character who we cheer for. And we don't cheer for characters who quit. We cheer for those who struggle. They don't have to win, but they must try.

Goals, obstacles and struggles. These are the ingredients that make stories come to life, and if you can decide what they are before you start writing, then you're already halfway towards creating something magical.

Ready to get started? Good. I think I can smell something bubbling away on the next page...

STORY PROMPT

MAGIC POTION

Write a story about a witch or a wizard making a magic potion. This is their goal, and I want you to decide why it is important to them.

What is the reason they need this potion, what spell do they want to cast? What ingredients do they need?

Once you've figured that out, add a nice, juicy obstacle or two (maybe they can't find a particular ingredient?), stir in a good dollop of struggle (how do they find that ingredient), then go and cast your spell (you know, write a story).

WRITE YOURSELF INTO A CORNER

CREATING CHALLENGING OBSTACLES FOR YOUR CHARACTERS

To be clear, this tip is not suggesting that you write *in* a corner. Although there is nothing wrong with doing so. Corners are snug, you have two walls to lean against if you become weary, and they tend not to have windows, which is good for cutting out distractions. But I digress – let's get back to the tip...

By "write yourself into a corner", I mean put your character in a difficult situation. One where it seems there is no way out for your hero. Create a problem – and this is the important part – where even you, the author, don't know the solution.

Because if you don't know how your character gets out of this pickle, then neither will your reader. And readers love that! So we tie our characters up, confront them with monsters, strand them in a wilderness and remove all hope. Just remember this: the tighter the corner we stuff our character into, the more satisfying it will be when they escape.

All you have to do now is find a solution to your character's "impossible" problem. It sounds daunting, I know, but trust me: there is always – *always* – a way out. And it's your job to find it. No one said writing is easy, but it sure is a lot of fun.

EXERCISE

GET YOURSELF INTO TROUBLE

Wait! Before you go smashing plates and drawing on the walls, I don't mean *that* kind of trouble. I want you – as discussed on the previous page – to write yourself into a corner! I want you to put a character in a situation where there is no obvious escape or solution. Perhaps they have been captured, maybe they are in trouble at home, could they be – literally – cornered by a wolf? Once you've got your character into a tough spot, I want you to help them find a way out. Get to it, and good luck!!

PUT THE WAND AWAY

DON'T GIVE YOUR CHARACTERS AN EASY WAY OUT

Yes, this book is all about adding magic to your stories. And yes, I've written an entire novel with a genie in it. But...

Try avoiding using too much magic in your stories. Even the ones with witches, wizards and genies. Why? Because our characters must struggle, and magic can often be the easy way out of a tricky situation.

Even Harry Potter doesn't rely on magic all the time. He and his friends rely more on their courage, brains and creativity to escape from peril. That's why they make such impressive heroes.

Solving a problem using non-magical methods requires you – the author – to be clever, inventive, surprising. It will make things more challenging for your character, but much more rewarding for your reader. So, put the wand away and think of something better instead.

The same goes for any easy fix used to get our characters out of trouble. Here are some to watch out for:

YOUR CHARACTER WAKES, REALIZING THE WHOLE THING HAS BEEN A DREAM.

A SHIP / AEROPLANE / POLICE CAR / FLYING SAUCER APPEARS OUT OF NOWHERE TO SAVE THE DAY.

A CHARACTER ALL OF A SUDDEN KNOWS KUNG-FU / BOMB-DISPOSAL / MEDICINE / HOW TO FLY A PLANE.

THE BADDIE FALLS DOWN A HOLE / FALLS ASLEEP / SLIPS ON A BANANA SKIN / IS CRUSHED UNDER A FALLING PLANT POT.

DEUS EX-MACHINA

The story cheats on the previous page and others like them are what we call Deus Ex-Machina.

The phrase goes back to ancient Greek theatre and means "God from the Machine". At the pivotal moment, a small crane would be used to lower an actor playing one of the Greek gods onto the stage. This god would then solve the story problems and bring the play to a convenient close.

Now, I'm not saying you should never use Deus Ex-Machina (you will find examples in many great books and movies such as *Lord of the Flies* and *The Wizard of Oz*). But I am saying, see if there's a better way first.

STORY PROMPT

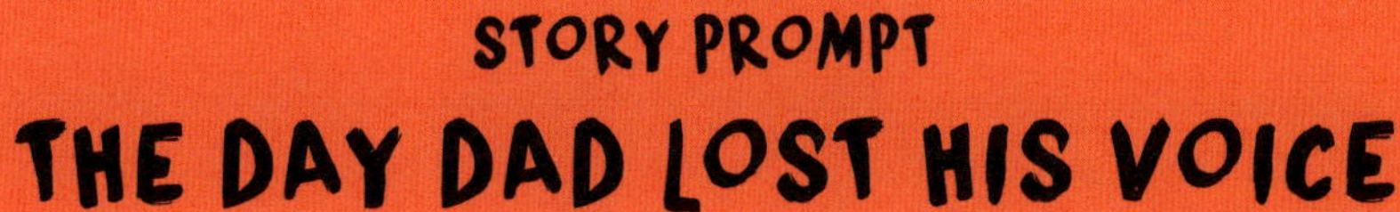

THE DAY DAD LOST HIS VOICE

You know what dads are like – always telling you to “eat your dinner!”, “do your homework!”, “don’t put your feet on the table!", “don’t tie all those balloons to your grandmother!” Well, what if someone’s dad lost his voice for a day and couldn’t tell them what to do? And – more importantly – what not to do?

Of course, this story will need an ending, and I imagine (but it’s not my story) that Dad will, somehow, get his voice back.

You have 30 minutes to do whatever you want. Anything, that is, except use Deus Ex-Machina.

DON'T LITTER!

CLEANING UP YOUR ADVERBS

I ***completely*** understand. You want your writing to be ***terribly*** exciting. You want your reader to know that a villain is ***remarkably*** big. That a teacher shouted ***angrily***. Or that someone was ***incredibly*** frightened. That they ***quietly*** whispered, "Help me". But be ***very*** careful. When we try to emphasize a particular quality, we can ***easily*** fall into the trap of cluttering our writing with a range of ***extremely*** overused words.

I'm talking, of course, about adverbs. And I am going to assume you know what adverbs are, so we can avoid having a grammar lesson (yeuuckk!).

Used sparingly and in the right places, adverbs can give our writing style and rhythm and draw attention to important points. But if we're not careful, adverbs can make our writing "lumpy" (just look at that opening paragraph!) and our stories slow.

I like adverbs and use them in *all* of my books. So before I send anything to my publisher, I go back through the manuscript and search for any messy and unnecessary adverbs.

Here is a list of twenty adverbs you can often cut from your writing:

And here are some of the ways I tidy up the adverbs in my own writing:

1. Vanish any silly adverbs

Some adverbs simply* aren't needed. In fact, they're kind of silly, like this one:

> She whispered **quietly**?

I mean, how else can she whisper? Certainly not loudly.

*This is an adverb, but it adds rhythm to the short sentence, so I'm keeping it.

2. Summon stronger words

Often, a single, powerful word can replace an adverb and the word it is modifying. For example:

Instead of: She was **incredibly frightened.**

Try: She was **terrified.**

3. Keep it simple

Sometimes, a simple statement of the facts can have all the impact you need. Particularly if you keep it short, and let it live on a line all of its own. Like this:

John opened the door.
"You John?" said the man standing on John's welcome mat.
The man was dressed in black, a hat pulled low over his eyes.
He was big.
"John?" said John. "No, I'm ... Dave."

I see that guy, and I don't need a modifier like "really" to understand just how big (and scary, because that's the point, isn't it?) he is.

4. Rewrite it

Instead of relying on an adverb to create an impression on your readers, rely on your creativity. Throw the adverb and the word it is describing out, and instead write a few words or a couple of sentences that will engage your audience's imagination. Read the following sentences and tell me which one is better (spoiler: it's the second one).

1. Samir was incredibly clumsy.

2. Samir was always bumping into things, dropping things and knocking things over. His father called him "Chaos on two legs", "The human wrecking-ball", "Samir the Smasher". But he called him these things fondly.

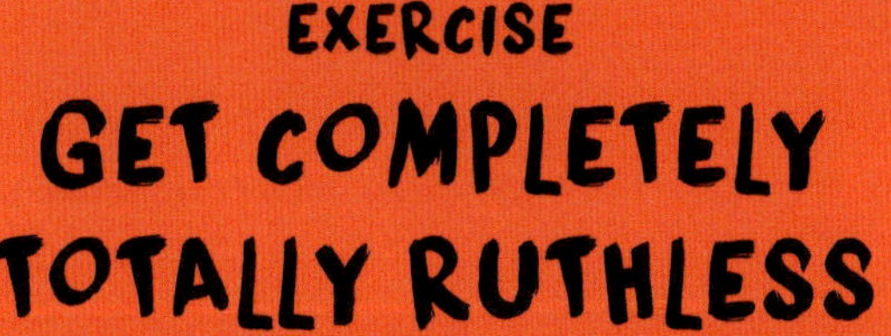

EXERCISE

GET COMPLETELY TOTALLY RUTHLESS

Right, I've given you four strategies for weeding adverbs out of your writing, so let's put them to the test. See if you can use those tips to rewrite the following phrases without using any adverbs. If you are trying Book One, Tip Four (and I hope you do), then you will need to write a few words or lines to set the scene, but that's why we're here, isn't it? To write!

- The rhinoceros was very, *very* big.
- The cat was incredibly pretty.
- My mum drove super fast.
- Her dog is extremely strong.
- Abraham is really funny.
- The man was a thoroughly bad person.
- My grandma's cooking is completely gross.

HOW BIG?

MAKING MEASUREMENTS MEANINGFUL

Ali was five feet and two inches tall.

Well, fine. The short sentence above tells us Ali's height, *exactly*. But it's a bit dull, isn't it? It doesn't create a particularly interesting picture in my mind. Because we don't see the world that way – in terms of feet, inches, centimetres or, for that matter, any other unit of measurement.

The situation is even worse when we're describing very big things. For example: The tower was 298 metres high.

I don't know about you, but I don't know what nine metres looks like, let alone 298! So instead of using these bland units of measure, let's describe people and objects in ways that reflect the way we see the world. Like this:

Harriet was just tall enough to reach the jam on the top shelf of the fridge, if she went on tiptoes.

The top of the tower brushed the undersides of the summer clouds. *Huh*, thought Elliott, *I guess that's why they're called skyscrapers.*

We can do the same for time:

The flight to Australia was four movies, one sleep, two meals, three wees, six hands of cards and one tantrum long.

Or weight:

The bathroom scales told Anwar he'd finally put on some muscle. Not much – he'd gained about the same weight as a beef burger without the bun – but it was a start.

So next time you want to tell your readers how long, tall, fast, heavy, small or large something is, instead of traditional units of measurement, reach for something more interesting – a description, metaphor, simile or comparison. You'll find them around 3,746% better.

EXERCISE

BIG FEET AND BLUE WHALES

Rewrite the statements below without using standard units of measurement. Write a few sentences if it helps you to unpack the object or thing we are describing – that is to open it up, look inside and find some interesting details to help us visualize it.

A good example of unpacking is the sentence on the previous page describing the length of a flight to Australia. So, put your ruler away, sharpen your pencil and describe the following:

- The average blue whale is around 30 metres long and weighs over 100 tons.
- The garden was 30 feet long and 20 feet wide.
- His feet were a size 10.
- The teacher shouted at 100 decibels.

AVOID CLICHÉS LIKE THE PLAGUE

KEEPING YOUR WRITING FRESH AND ORIGINAL

Clichés are overused phrases.* Like, well, like telling someone to avoid something like the plague. Or saying, "It's raining cats and dogs", or "I'm so hungry I could eat a horse!"

We use clichés because they're easy, and your readers will quickly understand what you are saying. But easy is rarely best. Because clichés are so common they often lose their impact and their descriptive power.

*Grown-ups use clichés all the time. Have you ever heard one say: "If I've told you once, I've told you a thousand times"? Or "You're making so much noise I can't hear myself think." Or "Your room looks like a pig sty"? Guess what? Clichés – every single one of them.

Let's take a closer look at this cliché:

"If I were you, Fiona, I'd avoid Donnie's Café like the plague."

We understand that the speaker is not a big fan of Donnie's Café, but we don't think much beyond this simple observation. So let's think about it now. Let's "unpack the cliché" – let's think about what it means, then use that information to write something funny, vivid and original.

In fourteenth-century England, a disease carried by fleas took the lives of roughly half the population. Victims developed boils and blisters. They died. And it was very contagious. So you avoided anyone, or anywhere, that had the plague. Because your life depended on it.

So, telling someone to avoid Donnie's Café "like the plague" is like saying: "If you value your health, Fiona, if you value your *life*, I'd stay well clear of Donnie's Café. I'd avoid it like a swarm of diseased fleas."

Now, you tell me, which is better?

Exactly. So if you want your writing to be fresh and interesting, avoid clichés like a cloud of fleas.

EXERCISE

CLICHÉS AS FAR AS THE EYE CAN SEE

I want you to pick three or four clichés, then see if you can improve them. But where will you find these clichés? Well, as luck would have it, I have prepared a massive list just for you. Try unpacking one, refreshing another and inventing something new to replace the third. Be brave, be creative and – last but not least – have fun!

Raining cats and dogs.

Like a breath of fresh air.

Fast as lightning.

Fit for a king / queen / princess.

Needless to say.**

**Then don't say it. Or do say it, but don't tell me it's needless.

Tip of the iceberg.

All hell broke loose.

A dazzling smile.*

*A dazzling simile would be preferable.

On thin ice.***

***Unless your character is, literally, on thin ice.

Defied all description.*
*I bet it doesn't. Give it a try.
WHAT'S YOUR BOOK ABOUT?
TO BE HONEST, IT'S VERY DIFFICULT TO DESCRIBE.

Too good to be true.
A CHANCE TO WIN A MILLION POTATOES...
WIN

Hanging by a thread.
UNRAVEL

Cunning as a fox.

As luck would have it.
KLANG!

An uphill battle.
THIS HAD BETTER BE WORTH IT.
TRUDGE

Had to be seen to be believed.
I'VE SEEN IT WITH SEVEN EYES AND I STILL DON'T BELIEVE IT.

Took her breath away.
BREATH
WHO'S STOLEN MY BREATH?

A face like thunder.

The calm before the storm.

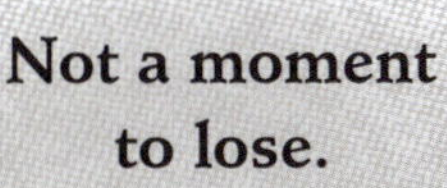

Not a moment to lose.

A flood of tears.

Against all odds.

As tough as nails.

WHAT ARE YOU LOOKING AT?

GRRR!

At the end of the day.

Shaking like a leaf.

One in a million.

Last but not least.

PORTMANTEAUS

WHY USE TWO WORDS WHEN YOU CAN CREATE A NEW ONE?

Nope, portmanteaus* (pronounced "port-man-toes") are not prehistoric fish. Rather they are a particular type of neologism.

And no, neologisms aren't prehistoric anythings either – they are (as you will know if you read *Unleash Your Creative Monster*) new or made-up words.

Portmanteaus are made by smashing two normal words together so they create a new word. For example, if you bang together the words *flatten* and *trample*, you get ...

Flample. As in:

> Poor Cho, he was flampled beneath a herd of helephants.

Helephants, by the way, comes from combining *hairy* and *elephants*.

Oh, and there's my dog, Bonnie. She's a *sproodle* – which is what you get when you cross a springer spaniel with a poodle.

*Originally, a "portmanteau" was the name for a suitcase with two sections. It was Lewis Carroll, author of *Alice's Adventures in Wonderland*, who first used the word the way we are using it today. In that book, he gave us the portmanteaus: *slithy* – made from "slimy and lithe"; and *mimsy* – from "miserable and flimsy".

Some portmanteau words have become so popular that we use them as part of our everyday language, like *Brexit* (*Britain* and *exit*); *hangry* (*hungry* and *angry*); and *frenemy* (*friend* plus *enemy*).

Some portmanteaus are joined by a shared letter, as in *helephants*. Others, like *brunch*, have a satisfying sound to the ear. There is no hard and fast rule when it comes to making portmanteaus, just have fun and use your judgement – or as I call it, fudgement.

EXERCISE
PORTMANTOWNS

Right, let's create some portmanteaus. Based on the suggestions below, see if you can make a few portmanteaus of your own – but let's call them portmantowns.

- Gardening in the rain
- A kiss and a hug at the same time
- Crying with laughter
- A double rainbow
- An urgent burp
- A satisfying sneeze
- An act of revenge involving a vegetable

LEVEL 2

WITCHCRAFT AND WIZARDRY FOR WRITERS

You know those tricks where someone pulls a rabbit from a hat, conjures a coin from thin air, or guesses your card? They're what I would call "basic magic". In writing terms, basic magic tricks are the kind discussed in the previous section.

But what about those large-scale tricks, like escaping from handcuffs, inside a sack, underwater, or making a 93-metre statue vanish?* This is high-level stuff practised by the most accomplished masters of magic.

Well – you guessed it, didn't you? – we're going to look at some high-level story magic in the next chapter. Master these tricks and you'll be a wizard of writing, a witch of words and an enchanter of the highest order.

*A magician called David Copperfield actually did this. The bookworms among you might have also noticed that this magician stole his name from a Charles Dickens character. What other proof do you need that writing is the ultimate magic?

SAVE THE DRAGON TILL LAST!

USING PROGRESSIVE COMPLICATIONS

Let's look at the bones* of a story:

Sir Shiny Pants the knight must rescue a princess. He leaves the castle and immediately fights a terrifying fire-breathing dragon. He is then attacked by a medium-sized bear. An old man hurls a rock at the knight and he is thrown from his horse. And finally, he is bitten by a mosquito. At which point, the princess sighs in disappointment and calls a taxi.

And the readers of this story know exactly how she feels – bored and disappointed. But why? We had a goal. We had loads of obstacles. And didn't Sir Shiny Pants struggle?

*The bones are the main story events. Then, when we actually write it, we add meat to the bones, "fleshing it out" and turning it into a strong story. Some people talk about "story beats". But I think "bones" sounds way cooler.

He did, but he struggled less and less as each obstacle became smaller than the last. And as the obstacles shrank, the story lost energy, fading out and ending with a whimper instead of a bang. This is what's known as an anti-climax. And you must avoid it at all costs.

You do this by making sure your character's obstacles become progressively bigger. As they grow, the excitement builds all the way to a dramatic finishing scene, known in story terms as a climax. Like this:

Our knight leaves the castle, he is attacked by a swarm of wasps, his horse throws him and gallops away, the knight hikes through a dense forest in his heavy armour, he has rocks thrown at him by a mad hermit and is attacked by a bear. Only now – exhausted, bashed and bruised – does he fight the enormous fire-belching dragon. And the princess, let me tell you, is impressed.

Now doesn't that feel like a story worth telling? Of course it does. Because as the story progresses, the problems grow, testing our character's determination, his courage and his skill, making him dig deep inside himself and making the audience cheer for him as he does.

STORY PROMPT

TARDY BRIAN

I want you to write a story about a character going to school in the morning. But here's the thing – this boy, Brian, is *always* late. He's a good kid; he just has a little trouble with timekeeping. And if he is late one more time, he'll have detention for a month. Will he make it in on time today? That's up to you. But whether he does or not, I want you to throw all kinds of problems at Brian starting from the moment his alarm clock goes off (or doesn't). But remember this – let the problems build from small to large.

Right, the clock is ticking, you'd better wake Brian up and get a move on.

WHAT CAN COMEDY TEACH US?

USING SET-UPS AND PAY-OFFS

Let's start with a joke:

> A bear walks into a café and says to the owner: "Can I have a cup of . . . . coffee, please?"
>
> To which, the shopkeeper replies: "Sure. But what's with the big pause?"

OK, maybe not the best joke in the world, but it demonstrates an important aspect of story-telling. The above joke – like most jokes – has two parts: the set-up and the pay-off.

The set-up tickles your curiosity and it makes you wonder what's going on or what will happen next.

The pay-off gives us a new piece of the puzzle – it might seem odd ("big pause"?) but when we look again at the set-up, (*it's a bear – bears have paws – "paws" sounds like "pause"!*) we make sense of the whole thing and feel all clever for getting it.

Stories use set-ups and pay-offs too. The difference is that in jokes, the set-up and pay-off are close together. In stories, they can be separated by many pages and chapters.

There are two types of story set-ups: Obvious Set-Ups and Sneaky Set-Ups. Let's look at the obvious kind first:

A ten-year-old boy wakes on Monday morning, goes to the bathroom, brushes his teeth, takes out a razor and shaves off his beard.

A boy with a beard! You can't help questioning a thing like that. These kinds of set-ups immediately grab our attention. They add suspense and intrigue to your story, making us race *forwards* looking for answers.

And then we have the sneaky kind:

A ten-year-old girl throws a tantrum and refuses to eat spaghetti bolognese at a friend's house, because it's been cooked with garlic.

Readers will remember this scene, but they won't find anything particularly unusual about it. After all, lots of children dislike garlic, and many can be rude. It's only later in the story, when the girl is revealed to be a vampire (this is the pay-off), that we look *back* at the incident and recognize the set-up.

Both set-ups – obvious and sneaky – end the same way. With a rush of understanding, a big smile and the words "Now I get it!"

Garlic is poisonous to vampires – that's why the girl had a tantrum! The boy, by the way, is a werewolf – that's why he shaves in the morning!

Say it with me: *Now I get it!*

Set-ups and pay-offs are great for creating intrigue in your story. But they are also a good trick for making exposition* interesting. The writer could simply state: "Billy was a werewolf." But by hinting at this idea with an earlier set-up, the effect of the reveal is hugely amplified.

*Don't worry if you've never heard of "exposition", we're going to talk about it on pages 58-61. And if you have heard of exposition – good for you!

SETTING UP AND PAYING OFF EMOTION

We've looked at how set-ups and pay-offs can add intrigue to a story and make exposition interesting. But we can also use set-ups to increase the emotional impact of certain scenes and events.

Imagine a girl wearing a pair of fancy earrings to a school disco. After a few dances, she realizes she has lost one of the sapphire studs. She's upset. *Really* upset. The girl goes on to explain that the earrings used to belong to her mother, and before that, her grandmother. More than that, the earrings were given to her grandmother by her grandfather. Who made them with his bare hands. From a sapphire that was given to him by *his* grandfather. Who had been given the sapphire by a princess. And so on.

This history – this emotional context – is all very interesting, only ... I don't know about you, but it doesn't affect me on a deep emotional level. Also, it's getting in the way of the business at hand – which is finding the earring!

It would be better if all of this history had been established earlier in a set-up...

Our character is turning eleven, and for her birthday, her mother presents her with a small blue box, inside of which are ... that's right, the sapphire earrings. Mum then goes on to explain the long and extraordinary history of these small sapphire studs. Then – maybe three or four chapters later – the girl loses the earrings.

It's the same information. But in this version the history enhances the birthday scene, building excitement around the gift. Then, at the disco, all that carefully set-up history *instantly* increases the emotional impact of the lost earring.

Just like a good joke, the secret of set-ups and pay-offs is all in the ... timing.

STORY PROMPT

THE AMAZING DOUBLE SET-UP

I want you to perform one of writing's most daring and astounding tricks – the double set-up in a single scene!

The first set-up:

Write a paragraph or two hinting at some interesting information about your character. For example: they are a werewolf, they are due to have a life-saving operation, or something else entirely.

The second set-up:

Write something telling us how a certain person or object is particularly important to them. It could be a piece of jewellery, a pet, a hat, a book.

Once you've written your double set-up, I want you to attempt the double pay-off! Write an emotional scene revealing the truth about your character, and how they react when something happens to their special something or someone.

It's a tough challenge. But if you've read pages 51–56 you're already set-up to succeed.

WHAT THE HECK IS EXPOSITION?

DELIVER IMPORTANT INFORMATION WITHOUT BEING BORING

Perhaps your story is set in the distant future, the ancient past, or on another planet. Maybe a character has a fear of spiders or the ability to talk with animals. Perhaps she is a princess, an orphan or a warrior, or (why not?) all of these things.

Exposition is the way we reveal (or expose) these important details that allow your reader to understand and enjoy a story.

When writing a story, we are usually working out the details as we go along, and there can be a temptation to blurt out all those details in the very first paragraph: the character's name, his age, the names and ages of his brothers and sisters and best friend. His hobbies and hates. What his parents do, what colour his hair and eyes are, and … you get the point.

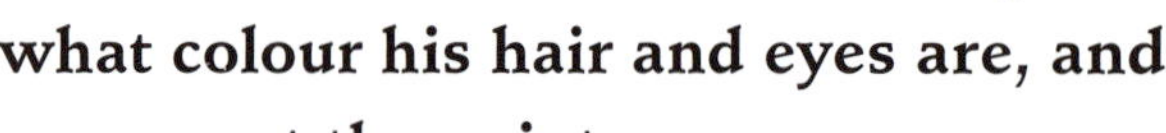

This is like showing your working when you do a maths problem at school. Teachers *love* to see the working. But readers of stories are more interested in the solution – that is, the story, the action, the next exciting scene.

So, by all means, work out the details as you go. But before you let them into your story, make sure that they are either important or interesting (or ideally both).

If you're not sure whether to include a piece of information in your story, use the awesome exposition supercomputer on the next page. OK, it's a flowchart, but it's still awesome!

THE AWESOME EXPOSITION SUPERCOMPUTER

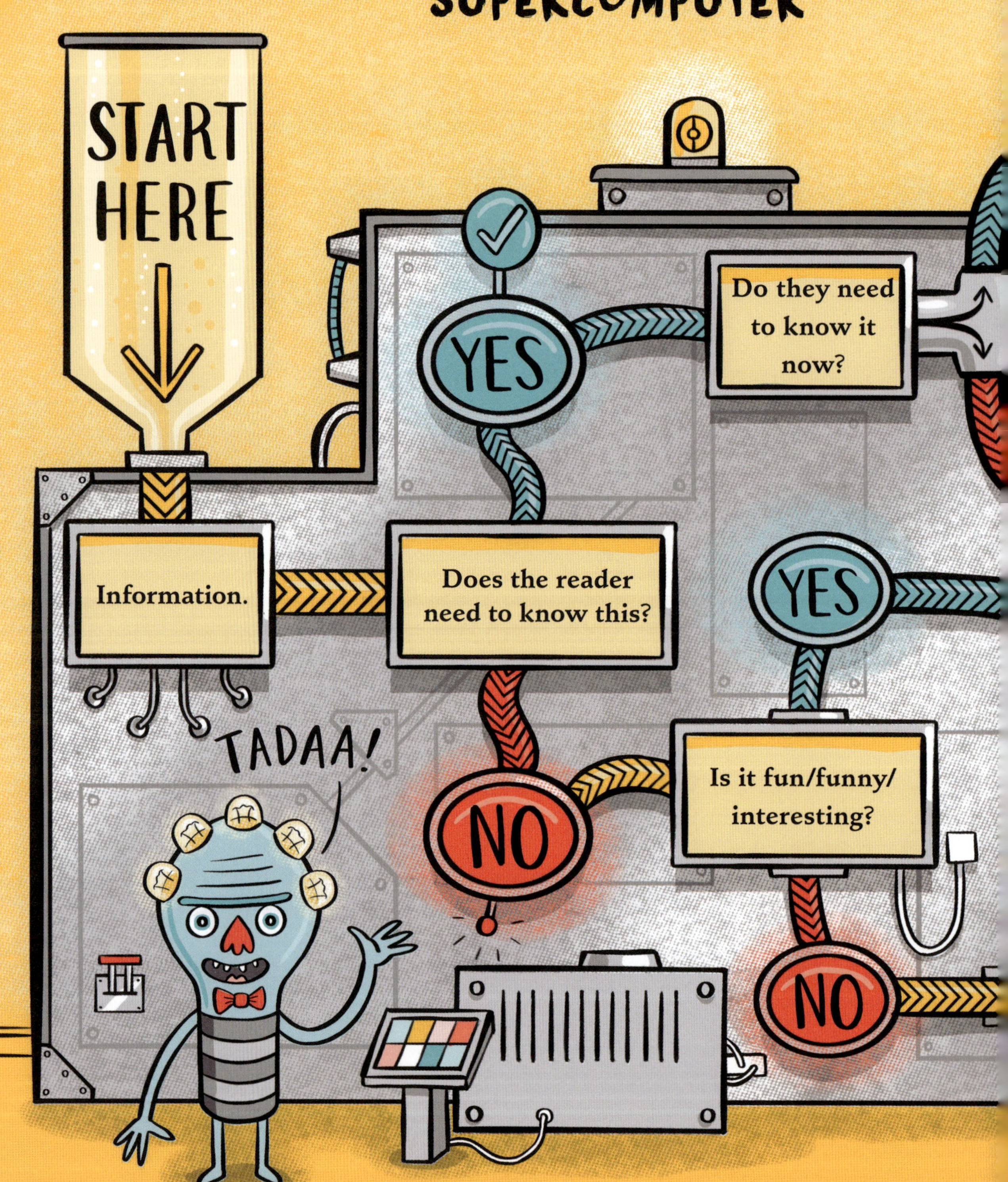

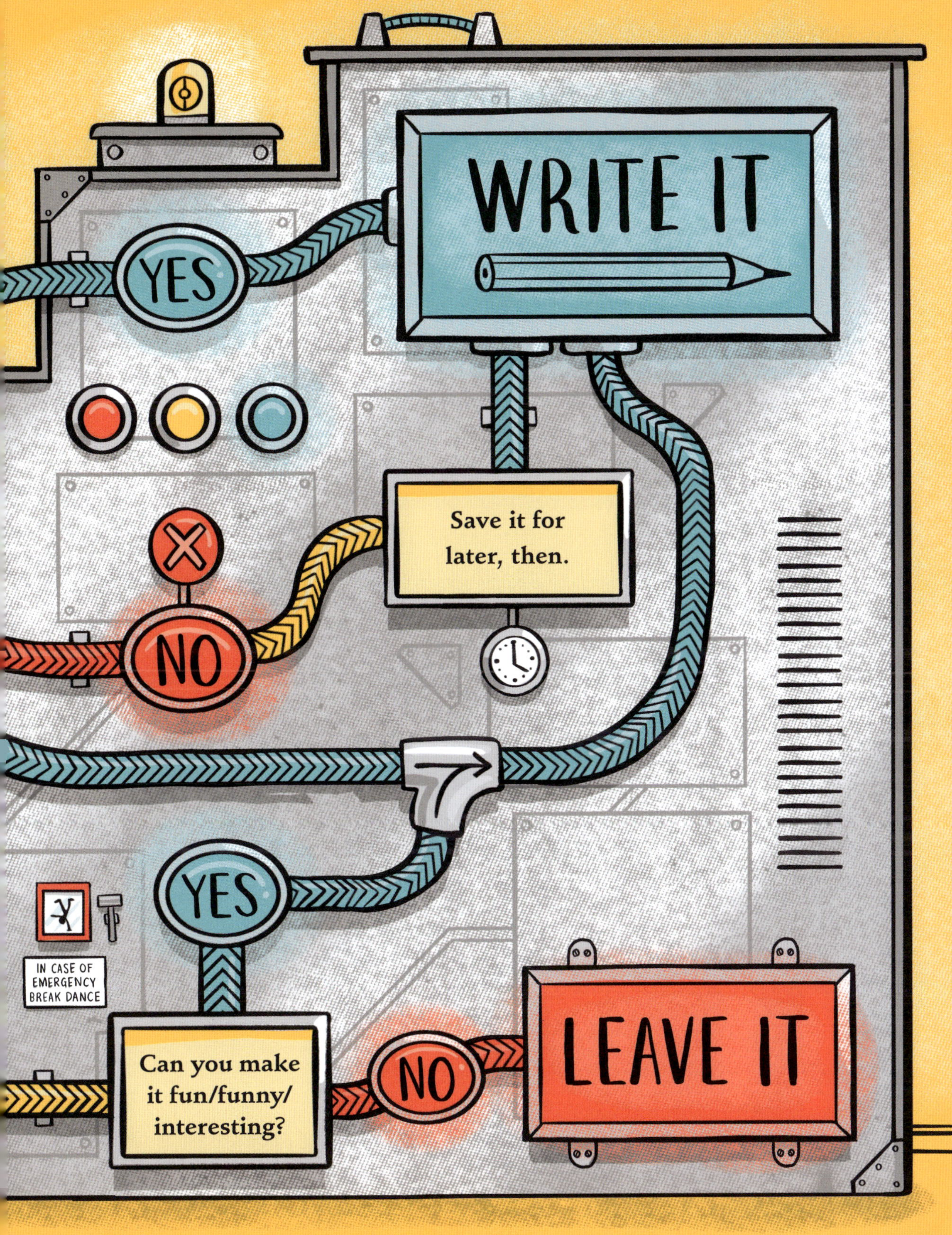
WRITE IT
YES
Save it for later, then.
NO
YES
IN CASE OF EMERGENCY BREAK DANCE
Can you make it fun/funny/ interesting?
NO
LEAVE IT

TWO TIPS FOR MAKING EXPOSITION INTERESTING

So, how do we reveal important information in an interesting way? The answer is: show, don't tell. Instead of simply telling the reader what they need to know, we show them. And if we do it well, they won't even notice. Here are two great ways of doing this:

1. Put it into action

Don't tell me a story is set in the future, show me the spaceships. Don't tell me someone is an orphan, show me the orphanage. Don't tell me someone is rich, show me their home...

The woman walked across the wide hallway, her footsteps echoing off the marble walls and high ceilings.

"Oliver," she called. "Oliver!"

Oliver didn't answer.

She walked into the dining room and checked beneath the table, but he wasn't there. She went through the library and into the cinema room. But no sign of Oliver in either. The same was true of the kitchen, the gym and the indoor swimming pool. Nothing else for it: she would have to check the bedrooms upstairs - all nine of them. Oliver wasn't allowed up there, but since when did a dog ever do what it was supposed to?

2. Turn your exposition into an argument

We often see exposition delivered in dialogue, but this can seem a little false – two characters telling each other things that each, presumably, already know. But if we turn it into an argument, then the exposition vanishes behind the action while sticking in your readers' minds. Here's an example.

Kaisha stormed into the kitchen, a pink jumper clutched in her fist.

"You've been wearing my clothes again, haven't you?"

Michael said nothing. He shook his head. Took another bite of his jam sandwich.

"Don't you lie to me, you little shrimp. I know you wore it because it's creased, it smells of boy and it's got jam on it."

"It was an accident," Michael pleaded. "Sorry, sis."

"No! Just because my mother married your father, that doesn't make you my brother or me your 'sis'! So stay out of my life and keep out of my room. Or else!"

Kaisha stormed out of the room. Michael shuddered and took another bite of his sandwich.

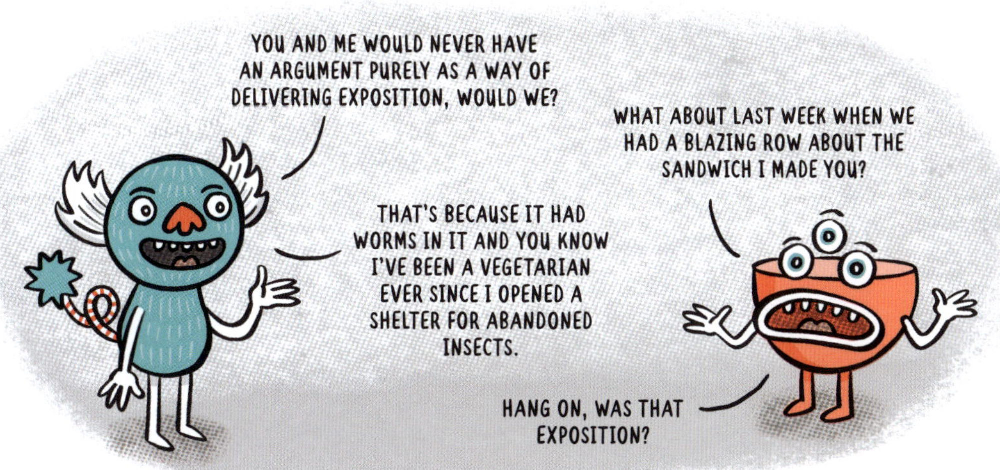

We've learned a lot of good story information in this short exchange: Kaisha is scary! Michael likes to wear her clothes. Also – and this is the important bit – Michael and Kaisha are step-siblings, thrown together because his father and her mother got married.

There is a third way to reveal important story information, but that belongs in another part of the book. If you want to read it again, skip back to the section called "Setting Up and Paying Off Emotion".

Right, I think it's time for an exposition exercise. Follow me to the next page...

STORY PROMPT

A SHORT TRIP TO THE DISTANT FUTURE

Write a scene set in the year 2222, with a character preparing for the day ahead. For example: taking a shower, eating breakfast, packing a bag. You will need to use your exposition skills to show we are in the future without telling us the year. Think about:

- How does the future look – the sky, the weather, the cities?
- What has been invented that doesn't exist now?

Remember, don't give your reader too much too soon, just a few details will do at this point.

Oh, and when you write this scene, let me know that your character is a criminal.

OK, off you go to the year 2222 – have fun!

BUT WHAT DO THEY *REALLY* MEAN?

ADDING SUBTEXT TO DIALOGUE

This is a very cool dialogue tip, which is easy to understand and easy to do. But it can greatly increase the impact of your writing. Subtext is what someone *really* means, but doesn't actually say when they are talking. Let's look at an example.

Chloe destroys Sophie's homework, getting her in big trouble at school. Sophie looks Chloe in the eye and says, very calmly, "I won't forget this."

What's the subtext? I think it's something along the following lines:

OK, maybe I went a *bit* far in my interpretation of Sophie's subtext, but that is the beauty of subtext – it engages the reader's imagination and puts them in the character's shoes (well, in their head, which is much more interesting than being inside a character's smelly trainers).

Why not try and add some subtext to your writing?*

**Subtext: You should definitely, 100% add some subtext to your writing. Do it now.*

STORY PROMPT

WHAT THEY'RE NOT SAYING

Jacinta asks her mother if bedtime can be one hour later. But her mother says, no, Jacinta needs her sleep!

So let's write a page or two of dialogue with added subtext. What is it our characters are suggesting but not saying?

Maybe Jacinta's friends tease her for having an early bedtime, but she is too embarrassed to say this to her mum. Your job is *hint* at the teasing subtext.

And how about Mum? Maybe Jacinta isn't doing too well at school and her mum thinks it's because her daughter is always tired, but she doesn't want to pressure Jacinta by telling her she is worried about her grades? That's her subtext.

As the dialogue escalates into an argument, you can have your characters finally say out loud what they mean. This will create a powerful moment of realization for your readers when – like the characters – they suddenly understand what was being suggested but not said.

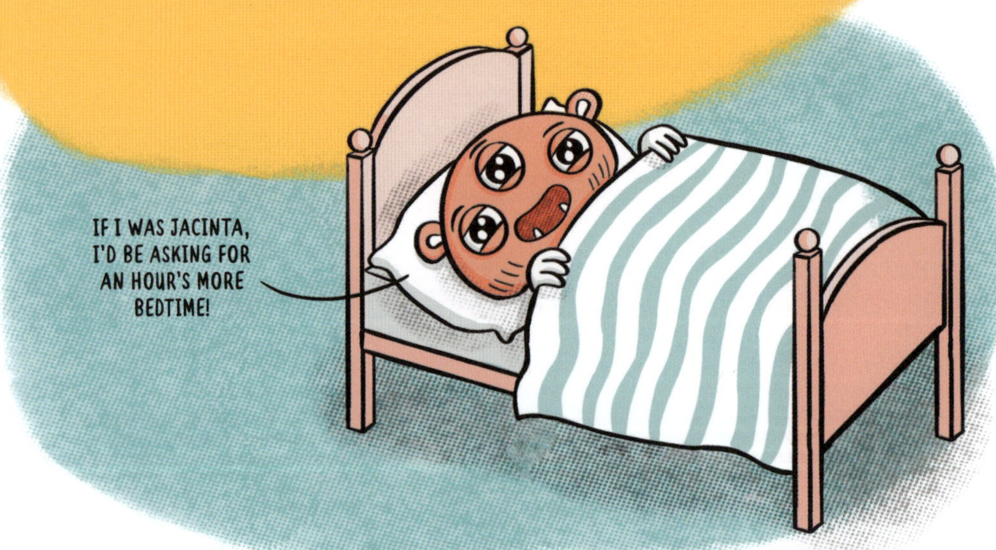

FORESHADOWS AND ECHOES

A TRICK FOR GIVING STORY EVENTS EXTRA IMPACT

Some of the best writing tricks affect the reader without them being aware of it. Like a kiss from a loved one while you're asleep – you may not notice it consciously, but you will certainly smile while you're dreaming. Foreshadowing works a little like that.*

Imagine an opening scene in a story: a man is adding a little ketchup to his bacon sandwich. Something distracts him, he squeezes the bottle too hard and squirts ketchup all over his clean white shirt.

On the surface, this is simply a scene about a man having a tough time making breakfast (we love our obstacles, after all). But on another level, the author is working her magic. She knows that later in the book, the man will walk under a ladder, a decorator will drop a tin of paint and the man will be covered from head to toe in thick, gloopy red paint.

*Although nothing has the magic of a kiss from a loved one.

When this big dramatic moment happens, the impact on the reader – even though they might not be aware of the magic at work – will be greater because of the earlier foreshadowing with the ketchup.

Echoes work in a similar way, although they travel backwards through the story. Like this:

Early in our story, a character might be involved in a car accident; perhaps she suffers an injury of some kind. Later, she sees a child playing with toy cars, smashing one into another. This later – completely non-dramatic – event echoes the earlier disaster, sending a shiver of recollection down the character's spine.

Foreshadowing uses something small to set up a later, more dramatic scene.

Echoes are small reminders of a significant and earlier event.

Foreshadowing mainly affects the reader.

Echoes tend to have a bigger effect on the character

Experiment with both in your next story and see how they can increase drama and create tension for your characters.

STORY PROMPT

A SMASH, A CRASH AND A NEAR MISS

I'm going to give you some dramatic scenarios below, and I'd like you to pick one of them and write a short – earlier – scene that foreshadows this.

Then write another scene that occurs later, echoing the same event.

If you like, you can write the big scene too.

Here are your dramatic scenarios:

- A boy is rushed to hospital with a broken leg after trying – and failing – to jump a stream on his BMX.
- One night in a storm, a tree is uprooted and comes crashing through the roof of a family home.
- A helicopter pilot is flying above a city when the engines fail. He almost crashes but manages – just – to land the craft in the middle of a lake.

FAKE-OUTS

MANIPULATING TENSION* AND BUILDING DRAMA

As writers, we want our stories to be interesting enough that readers are continually guessing what's going to happen next. But we want them to guess wrong. Because if they guess correctly, then our story is in danger of becoming predictable. And predictable is bad news for stories.

Let's look at a short scene:

> A man is being chased by a savage wolf, and his only means of escape is across a frozen lake. He steps onto the ice ... it creaks, but it holds. He takes two, three, four more steps then stops when a small crack appears at his feet. The wolf is at the edge of the lake, snarling and drooling saliva. There is no going back now, so the man edges further across the ice.
>
> There is another creak. Another crack. In desperation the man begins to run. The ice shatters and he drops into the lake's freezing depths.

Not bad. But I bet you saw it coming, didn't you? And if your entire story is built from scenes like this, then your readers will soon lose interest.

*A fancy way of saying "mess with the reader's head".

So let's add a fake-out.

The man steps onto the ice. It creaks. It cracks. But the man must continue, so this is exactly what he does. He takes three more steps, there is an ear-splitting creak and the ice cracks around his feet, forming a pattern like a vast spider's web of doom. The ice breaks. But before he is plunged into the freezing water, the man grabs a low branch from an overhanging tree. He's saved! And then the branch snaps. And the man drops into the icy depths.

The branch was the fake-out. It made you think – just for a moment – that the man was going to make it. And then – tricked you – he takes a very cold bath.

NOTE: A fake-out is different from a reversal of fortune. That happens when someone's situation goes from good to bad. Or bad to good. The man successfully crossing the lake, for example.**

A fake-out is sneakier than that. It goes from bad to good then back again. Or good to bad then back to good. It zigs, then it zags. That's what catches the reader out. That's what stops your scene from being predictable.

**Screenwriters refer to fake-outs as "reversals". But I find this term confusing as it's similar to "reversal of fortune". I just thought you'd like to know!

TWO FAKE-OUTS TO USE IN YOUR WRITING

Two common forms of fake-out are the false alarm and trick ending. If you like movies, you will have seen them a hundred times, but they can work just as well in written stories.

Here's a false alarm:

A man wakes in the middle of the night, he hears a creaking sound downstairs. Maybe something growls. There is a storm outside, making it hard to tell. But this is monster country, so the man is understandably scared. As he searches the house, we build the tension – maybe the lights go out, a shadow flits past a doorway. And just when we are sure the guy is going to get got … a cat pads up to him, nuzzles his leg and pads away. Relief! It was a false alarm. And just as we relax … the man is attacked by a monster.

The cat was the false alarm and we used it to trick the reader into thinking everything was OK, so that when the bad thing did happen, the shock hits even harder.

And here's a fake ending:

> A woman battles a killer robot from the future (hmm, sounds like an idea for a great movie). There is a great deal of chasing, hiding and bashing but the robot just keeps on coming. Until … the woman jams a bomb into the robot's metal ribs and – *boom!* – blows the thing to bits. Our hero is saved. Or so we think! Half of the robot – the half with a head and arms – makes one final grab for the woman's throat. But this woman is a clever cookie. She has lured the robot into the path of a metal-crushing machine. She hits the button and flattens the killer robot. *Now* she's safe.

The robot exploding was a fake ending. And just like the false alarm, it is a way of manipulating tension and making the viewer, or the reader, believe everything is going to be OK. When, in actual fact, everything is far from OK!

And that's all I have to say about false alarms and fake endings.*

*Actually, this is another fake ending. There's an exercise on the next page. See you there.

STORY PROMPT

THE CABIN IN THE WOODS

Fake endings and false alarms are common in scary movies, so let's write one for a scary story. Write a story involving two characters taking a holiday in a cabin located deep in the woods (horror stories love a cabin in the woods!). One of your characters hears a noise outside, so they go to investigate. This is your chance to write a false alarm. And then, when the real monster is revealed, I want you to write a false ending. And of course the real ending.

Off you go, and stay safe!

CREATING
MAGICAL
CHARACTERS

CREATING MAGICAL CHARACTERS

The next section is not about creating witches, wizards, elves, fairies, genies and other magical folk.* It's about creating vivid characters that feel real and alive, which is a magic all of its own.

*You can, of course, also use these tips to create witches, wizards, elves, fairies, genies and other magical folk.

STORY IS CHARACTER

There's a saying about writing that I like. I like it so much I made it the heading of this page: "Story is Character".*

It means that at the heart of a story – beyond the explosions, car chases and adventure – lies character. All the other stuff is simply there to test our character, to help or hinder them in achieving their story goal.

That goal, by the way, begins with character too. And how our hero reacts to the obstacles in her path, that also depends on character.

Sometimes you will build a character to inhabit the story idea you have invented. Other times, you will begin with an interesting character and build a story around them.

Character is important. So the next section is dedicated entirely to that. We'll look at how to build them, make them real and how to make every character (genie or otherwise) magical.

*"Character" has two similar but subtly different meanings. On one hand, it means a person in a story. On the other, it means someone's personality. To put it another way: characters have character. Or at least they should.

WHO'S TELLING?

CHOOSING A POINT OF VIEW FOR YOUR STORY

Before you start writing a story, it's worth thinking about who is going to tell it. Sure, you have a hero, but is she the best person to tell the story? The stories of Sherlock Holmes (the world's greatest detective) are not told by Sherlock, but by his companion, Dr Watson. Why?

Sherlock is a genius and sees clues other people would miss. If the readers knew what Sherlock knew, the story would lose much of its mystery. But because Dr Watson – the teller of the tale – is less informed, so is the reader. And that makes the story more interesting.

So don't assume your hero has to be the voice of the story. Think about who has the most interesting point of view. Maybe it's a best friend, or a pet. Perhaps it's the villain of the story.

Most stories can be told from several* viewpoints, you just have to decide which one is the best fit for yours.

*And some are told from multiple viewpoints.

STORY PROMPT

THE EXPLORER, THE GUIDE AND THE JUNGLE

Let's write a story about an explorer searching the Amazon jungle for rare plants. The obvious point-of-view character would be the explorer.

But what about an Indigenous tribesman from the jungle who is acting as her guide? Seen through his eyes, with limited knowledge of her culture, the story would be very different.

Or how about telling the story from the viewpoint of the jungle itself? Does the jungle feel threatened by this explorer? Is it protective of its plants and wildlife? And is there anything it can do to slow her down and scare her off?

So, pick a viewpoint and explore how it affects your story.

WHY BOTHER?
MOTIVATING YOUR CHARACTERS

We've talked about the importance of giving your character a goal, and then making them struggle to overcome the obstacles you place in their path. But why should your character put up with all of that hassle?

You might think it would be fun to make your character climb Mount Everest, for example, but what's in it for them? We call this our character's motivation.

"To get to the top?" might be a good reason for you or me to climb a mountain, but it doesn't make for a great story. Why? Because if that's your character's only motivation, they will simply give up and go home as soon as the going gets tough. And because this is a story, the going must get tough.

However, if their reason is to win a £5,000 prize, then – when our character encounters a snowstorm and an avalanche – he might *think* of quitting, but ultimately he will persevere because of the prize money.

But say he breaks his leg and has to cross a frayed rope-bridge. Will he really risk his life for a few thousand pounds? Probably not.

Unless … unless his daughter has been kidnapped and he needs the money to pay the ransom. Now – broken leg and rickety bridge or not – giving up isn't an option for our character.

So, after you give your characters a goal, and before you start throwing obstacles at them – be sure to give them a good reason to accept the challenge. Your characters will be more resourceful and more heroic for this motivation. And your stories will become more exciting and satisfying, which should be more than enough motivation for you.

EVERYONE WANTS SOMETHING

MAKING MINOR CHARACTERS WORK

We've already established that the hero of your story wants something. That's what "story" is, after all – a character overcoming obstacles in order to achieve a goal. That goal might be to play rugby for their country, to escape from danger, to form a rock band or to win the heart of someone they love.

But what about the supporting characters? Don't they want something too?

Think of the people in your life – your friends, family, that teacher who's always grumpy. They all want something, don't they? It could be a holiday, a new boyfriend, a new job, or a really big axe. Everyone wants something, even it's nothing more than a cup of coffee.

So give some of your supporting characters something to want too. It will make them appear more lifelike. It will motivate them to act – to do something – rather than just sitting on their bums. And when characters act, the story becomes more interesting. Particularly when the thing one character wants gets in the way of the thing another character wants. When this happens we have conflict, tension, drama, comedy. And all of that stuff is good stuff.

I'll show you what I mean on the next page…

STORY PROMPT

LET'S GO BANANAS!

Evil genius Kevin has created a device that allows him to control the brains of chimpanzees. He plans on using this technology to turn the chimps into jewel thieves.

Secret agent Ruby is speeding towards Kevin's lair with a wagon full of bananas. Because even brainwashed monkeys can't resist a ripe banana.

Sitting beside Ruby is her sister, Evie. But while Ruby drives, Evie looks out of the window. She's not affecting the story at all.

So let's give Evie something to want. Maybe …

Evie is *bursting* for a wee and wants Ruby to stop so she can take a tinkle in the bushes. Ruby wants to keep driving.

Ruby and Evie argue. Perhaps Evie grabs the steering wheel. And if she does, then what? Whatever happens this scene has become a lot more enjoyable just because Evie now wants something.

So, over to you. Ruby is driving, Evie is bursting, and we have 30 minutes before Kevin releases the chimps. Get writing!

RUBBER DUCKIES

GIVING YOUR CHARACTER A BACKSTORY

In many stories there is a scene where the villain, or the hero, explains what made them the way they are. Why they are so brave, or greedy, or vengeful, or downright wicked. This is called their backstory.

Or, as one American writer called it – their "rubber ducky". That writer was Paddy Chayefsky,* a legendary screenwriter who won three Oscars** for his movie scripts.

When talking about backstory, Mr Chayefsky used the example of someone stealing a little boy's rubber ducky. Then, following this traumatic experience, the boy grows up full of anger and becomes, for example, a deranged maniac.

*Pronounced: Ch-eye-eff-ski

**The Oscars are like the Olympics for movies. Winning one is more than most people could dream of. Winning three is crazy!

Knowing a character's backstory will help you to make them realistic, it will help you decide on their goal, why they are chasing it and what obstacles will most challenge them. If a character was bullied as a child, for example, this might affect how they act as an adult. And a character who grew up in poverty will see the world differently from one who was surrounded by wealth and privilege.

But whilst backstory is useful for the writer, Paddy Chayefsky warns us to use it cautiously. We don't have to reveal it *all* to our readers. And we certainly don't need to reveal it all at once. I think Mr Chayefsky's main objection was to those scenes where a villain delivers a grand speech about his rubber ducky just before executing his evil plan. Those scenes often feel a bit fake. A bit – I suppose – *plastic*.

Personally, I love a good rubber ducky story, and several James Bond movies wouldn't be the same without them.

So do get to know your character's backstory and do use it to drive your story. And try to find a clever or satisfying way of revealing it your reader, instead of just having your character blurt it all out in one go.

Get it right, and maybe one day you'll win an Oscar of your own.

STORY PROMPT

KEVIN'S DUCKY

Remember our evil genius from the last story prompt?

Of course you do. Who could forget a villain with an army of jewel-thieving brain-controlled chimpanzees? Exactly – no one.

But why is Kevin the way he is? Why is he evil? Why monkeys? Why jewels? Write a scene from Kevin's childhood explaining how the little boy became the evil genius.

BADDIES NEED LOVE TOO

CREATING MAGNIFICENT VILLAINS

Everybody loves a hero (and now I really do mean the kind with muscles, perfect teeth and twenty ways to kick a bad guy's butt). We love their courage and cunning, their skill and strength, their gadgets and their great hair. Why? Because that's how the writer wrote them. Writers give goodies friends, family and all the best lines.

But what about the villains, the mad scientists and other wrong-doers? Too often, writers neglect their baddies. But this is a mistake. The best stories have the best characters – the good *and* the bad. So value your villains, breathe life into your baddies, adore your abominable creations.

Give them impressive skills, exciting interests and unusual tastes. Give them someone to love, give them their own problems to overcome. Make them clever or funny. Allow then to appreciate art, or play the violin like a master. Make them interesting. And not just because your readers and your story deserve it.

A hero is only as impressive as the obstacles she overcomes. The bigger the challenge she faces, the braver she is. Anyone can overcome a half-witted, clumsy, cowardly baddie. But it takes a real hero to vanquish a powerful villain.

Like I said, everyone loves a hero. But as a writer, it's your job to love your villains too.

PROJECT
CREATING A CHARACTER PORTRAIT

When writers talk about a character portrait, they mean a portrait of words: details describing things like the character's interests, appearance, job, fears, hopes, skills, backstory and (metaphorical) mask.*

When it comes to writing the story, the author may not use everything from this portrait of words, but in jotting all this down they are sure to come up with a few surprises that will help shape their story.

*You can learn more about masks in the section of that name (page 106).

EVIL GENIUS'S EVIL TWIN

EVIL TWIN'S MUTTLY CREW

So let's create a character portrait. Only I want you to actually draw your character, and then add labels describing aspects of their personality. Oh, and let's make them a magnificent villain, shall we?

LOOKS LIKE HIS BROTHER WAS ALSO BARKING MAD.

When writing your labels, think about the things listed above – job, goal, interests, fears and so on – but also consider any interesting aspects of your drawing. Does your character have any noteworthy physical characteristics? Interesting hair, big muscles, tired eyes? Are their clothes fancy or ragged? And if so, why?

Oh, and give them a name. And when you're done with that, see if you can create a story that will allow your character to come to life.

ONE HEAD IS BETTER THAN THREE

COMBINING MINOR CHARACTERS

Sometimes when we write, our pages fill up with characters quicker than they fill with story. We introduce the main character, her parents, her brothers, her three best friends, a couple of teachers, a nemesis and a mysterious pigeon.

But do we really need all of these minor* characters? A story is a finely balanced machine: every word counts and every character must earn their keep. We can't have random characters cluttering up the place and getting in the way.

So instead of three friends, ask yourself: Can I combine silly Sajid, daring Dave and funny Fiona into a single, funny, brave and silly BFF?

*Characters other than the main character.

Do I need a smelly music teacher and a scary PE teacher? Or can it be one smelly *and* scary teacher who takes both subjects?

Maybe the answer to these questions is no, I need them all – in which case, trust your instincts and carry on. But think carefully before you rule out the idea of squishing two or more characters into one. Because if you can reduce the headcount in your story, you will achieve two important things:

- It will be easier for your readers to keep track of who's who.
- Your characters will become more interesting.

Or, to combine these reasons into one single reason:

- Your story will be better.

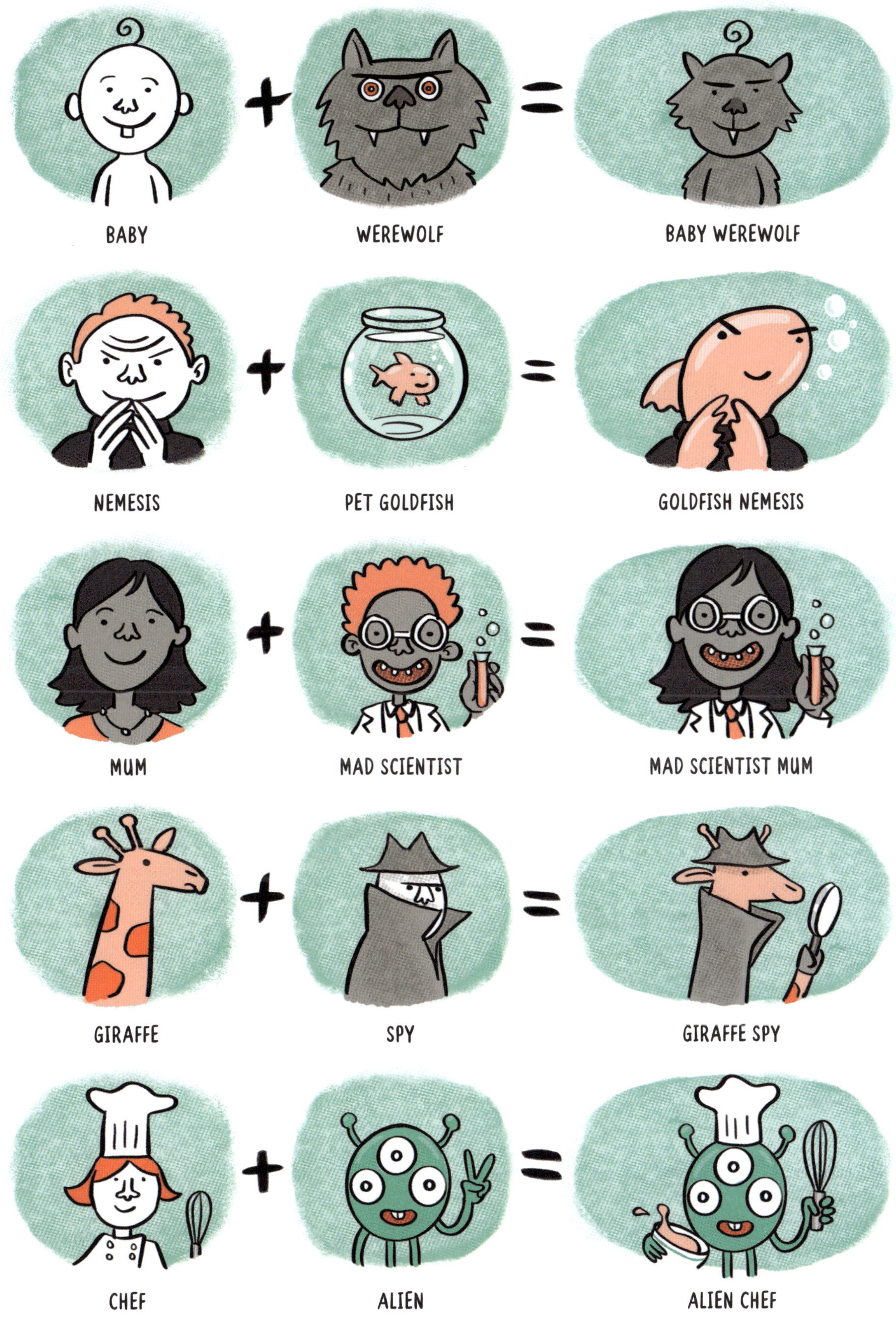
BABY
WEREWOLF
BABY WEREWOLF
NEMESIS
PET GOLDFISH
GOLDFISH NEMESIS
MUM
MAD SCIENTIST
MAD SCIENTIST MUM
GIRAFFE
SPY
GIRAFFE SPY
CHEF
ALIEN
ALIEN CHEF

STORY PROMPT

TWO-HEADED EDDIE

We've been talking about combining different characters to keep a story from getting confusing and overcrowded, but it's given me an idea. What about combining two very different personalities in a single, two-headed character? The two heads can't agree on anything – where to go, what to do, what to eat. It would be a massive headache. A double headache, in fact.

I want you to write a scene with the two heads arguing over what they are having for supper.

Oh, one more thing I probably should have mentioned: Eddie is a dragon. And one of the heads has just spotted a very delicious-looking knight.

VOICES, UMS AND FIDGETS

GIVING DIALOGUE CHARACTER

Everybody speaks differently. We have different accents for a start, not just from other countries, but from different regions within a country. Some people talk fast, and others slow. Some use fancy language, and others use rude words. Some are loud, and others whisper. We call all of this the character's *voice*.

People also have specific dialogue traits – little noises and sounds, words or phrases they overuse. Think of "um"s and "er"s and "hum"s and "hah"s. Maybe someone says "hmm" a little too often, and someone else is fond of the word "wicked".

Does a character clear their throat frequently? Do they hesitate or gesticulate?* Do they click their fingers when thinking of the right word? Do they use sign language?

Pay attention to the way people speak in everyday life, and use your observations to colour the way your characters talk.

When it comes to voice, a little variety goes a long way – a few dialogue traits for a couple of key characters will be plenty. We don't want an entire cast of characters all coughing and clicking, hmming and hahing, and using unusual words.

Although that does sounds kind of fun, now that I think of it.

*"Gesticulate" means using your hands to help express yourself.

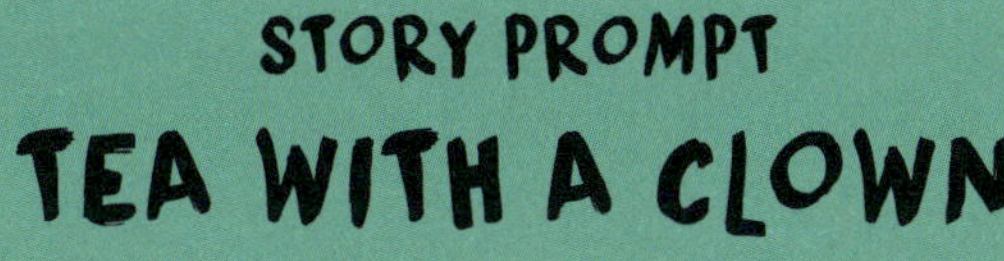

STORY PROMPT

TEA WITH A CLOWN

One of the trickiest things to write is a dinner party scene because you have to make sure all the characters get to speak and that the reader keeps track of who's who. Making sure everyone's voice is different will help you achieve this.

So let's write a dinner party scene, but to make it a bit more interesting let's set it in ... a circus! How about a clown, a trapeze artist and a strongman? Or perhaps you want to invite some different guests.

What are they talking about? Maybe they think one of the acts is letting the circus down. Or maybe someone is thinking of running off and getting a "sensible" job, in a bank, or as a doctor?

Think about the words the characters use, the noises they make, any hesitations, anything they do with their hands.

Voices are sure to be raised during this exchange. Just make sure that each of these voices is different.

MASKS

THE CHARACTER WE SEE AND THE PERSON UNDERNEATH

Have you ever worn a scary mask at Halloween? Isn't it funny that as soon as we put a mask on, we start acting differently? We become someone else.

People do this kind of thing more often than you might realize – not with monster masks, but with metaphorical masks.

SOMEONE MIGHT WEAR

So to help our characters feel more realistic, we give them masks – making them appear a certain way before magically revealing their deeper personality.

Some character masks are deliberate – a character chooses, for example, to hide their fear behind a mask of toughness. But sometimes the character is not aware they are hiding some part of themselves. Their mask (of rudeness, say) may be something that has developed over time, without the character realizing.

Now here's the important part – at some point in your story, the mask must slip and reveal the true character behind. Otherwise, how will we know it was a mask?

But don't drop your character's mask all at once. Instead, give your reader little hints of what lies behind the bully, the joker, the brat. Show us glimpses of your character's true personality, before – in an emotionally satisfying and revealing scene – we drop the mask once and for all.

When you're writing, use character masks to bring your stories to life.

And when it's Halloween, use rubber masks to frighten your friends to death.

EXERCISE

BUILD A CHARACTER THEN HIDE THEM

I want you to create a character who hides part of their personality behind a mask. Start by building the underlying character – give them some traits, maybe a goal or an ambition. Decide what they're good at and what is their greatest fear.

Once you've done all of that, you're going to give them a mask. You will also need to decide why they are wearing it. What caused this character to hide a part of themselves away? If you can answer that, you'll have more than a character. You'll have a story. So why not write that too?

ICE CREAM OR CHOCOLATE CAKE?

GIVE YOUR CHARACTERS A DILEMMA

As you know, a fundamental part of storytelling is making your characters struggle. We do this by placing "obstacles" in their path. Physical obstacles like dragons and floods, personal obstacles like a lack of confidence and resource problems like a lack of time or money.

But there is an entirely different form of obstacle that is sure to torment your characters and delight your readers. It's the dilemma – otherwise known as a tricky choice between two (or occasionally more) options.

Dilemmas can be between two bad options, or two good ones.

Remember our character who was being chased through a forest by a wolf?* His dilemma was whether to confront the wolf, or take his chances with the thin ice. This kind of dilemma is a choice between the lesser of two evils.

*You'll find him on the section called "Fake-outs" on pages 72–74.

Or how about a dilemma between the greater of two goods? For example, being invited to two parties at the same time on the same day. Or the choice between chocolate cake and ice cream?

Dilemmas are a great way to add intrigue and tension to your stories. But they do something else – they reveal the hero's true character. After all, it's easy for someone to say they're brave – but it's a different thing altogether when they have to prove it.

One more dilemma to explain:

A boy sees someone being bullied on the way home from school. The bully is big, nasty and ruthless. The victim is half the bully's size and terrified. They are on a bridge spanning a lake. The bully is forcibly removing the kid's shoes, and it looks like he is planning on throwing them into the water. The boy who sees all this is about to become the hero of our story, and he has two choices:

1. Confront the bully. This is dangerous and frightening – he will almost certainly get thumped. He might also have *his* shoes thrown in the lake. Maybe both.

2. Do nothing. This is the safe option and means he won't get thumped. But it also means allowing an innocent victim to suffer.

The choice, ultimately, will come down to the character. Are they brave, frightened, foolish, sensible, hot-headed? It's a heck of a dilemma, and it's also a pretty good start to a story. So why don't we write it?

STORY PROMPT

THE BULLY ON THE BRIDGE

Start this story at the point when our hero notices the bully removing the other boy's shoes. And then decide how our hero is going to handle this particular dilemma.

Whatever you choose, I'd like to suggest that your character later regrets their decision. Why? Two reasons:

First, it gives your character another obstacle to deal with, namely self-doubt. They must question their decision and wonder whether there was a better way of handling the situation.

Second, it gives your character a chance to learn a lesson and grow as a person. They can go from being scared to brave. From foolish to cunning. Or some other transformation.

For this growth to happen, you will need to write a scene where the character is faced with yet another dilemma. Maybe it's the same as the first, or maybe something new. But it must give your character an opportunity to act on the lessons he or she has learned. And to reveal a new side to their character.

What will your character do?
It's time to decide.

WHEN THE MAGIC ISN'T HAPPENING
5:00

IT'S GOOD TO GET STUCK

No one is awesome at something overnight. Except my aunt Fran, who woke up one morning suddenly knowing how to play the bagpipes.* It takes time and perseverance to learn a new skill, and with very few exceptions, the first time anyone tries anything, they will be rubbish at it. They will *stink*. And that's awesome. Why? Because you are challenging yourself; you are – like the hero in a story – embracing struggle. Yes you will get stuck. Yes there will be days when it feels as if the magic just isn't happening. But getting stuck isn't failing. Getting stuck is the first step in learning and growing.

The trick to improving is simple – you keep turning up. You go to another netball practice, another bagpipes class, another rehearsal. And over time, you will magically get better, then good, then great.

This section contains tips and ideas for those days when writing seems like a struggle. So try these ideas and keep turning up. Because (unlike my aunty Fran) you can definitely do it.

*Well, she said she knew how to play them, but to be honest the noise was almost unbearable.

JUMP AROUND

AND WRITE THE NEXT INTERESTING SCENE

If you're stuck in the middle, or even at the start of a story, a good trick is to think about the ending. Will the good guy win or lose? Do your characters fall in love or fall out? Is it a happy ending or sad? Will there be a battle, a party, an explosion, an invasion of aliens?

Then, having decided how your story will finish, write that ending. You can go back to the middle later, but the process of setting the ending down will give you a destination to aim for.

This trick isn't limited to endings either. If you get stuck on one particular scene, just jump to another. Maybe you know there will be a custard-pie fight later in your story – well write it now, then go back and fill in the gaps later.

Or maybe you're excited to write a scene where your hero has to wrestle a giant octopus. Do it now, and later you can worry about what comes earlier. The trick is to keep your fingers (and your brain) moving. Because while you're writing a scene that belongs later in your story, your brain will often figure out how to fix whatever it was that had you stuck. Brains are good like that.

STORY PROMPT

OCTOPUS FIGHT!!!

Sometimes we have an idea for a scene that doesn't necessarily have a story attached to it. But that thing is so exciting we just have to write it. Well, the idea of wrestling an octopus on the previous page is exactly one of those things. So let's write it now. Write a scene with a character wrestling a great big slippery eight-limbed creature. And who knows, if you ask yourself *why* this is happening, you might even get a story out of it.

INTERVIEW YOUR CHARACTERS

A TRICK FOR MAKING CHARACTERS FEEL REAL

Now this next tip might sound a bit … out there, a bit bonkers, but here it is. I want you to sit down and talk to one of your characters.

What's that you say? Your characters aren't *real* people.

To which I say, maybe not, but they should *feel* real. To you and your readers.

One way to make our characters real is by giving them a life beyond the limits of the story you are writing. But before you can do that, you have to get to know your characters, to understand them. So have a conversation with them – out loud if you like, or written down like lines of dialogue.

If your character is an adult, ask about their childhood. If he or she is a child, ask what they want to do when they grow up. Ask them what music they like, what games they play, what they had for breakfast and the name of their best friend. Ask them to tell you a joke or sing you a song. What are their dreams and nightmares?

And don't forget the important stuff: why they are so determined to become a ghost hunter, cook for the queen, sail around the world, or pursue any other goal you create for them.

If you don't understand your characters, they will be no more than puppets on the page, simply going where you point them and doing whatever it is you command them to do.

But once you get to know them, their actions have purpose and meaning. They will begin to question your instructions and make surprising decisions of their own. They will, in other words, become real, which is one of the greatest tricks a writer can pull off.

PROJECT

DEAR YOU

Dear Writer,

I want you to write a letter or postcard to yourself from one of your characters. If they're a spy, perhaps they have been captured and the note is a plea for help. Are they a child like you, grounded and writing from their bedroom? Maybe it's a postcard from the past or a letter from the future. Let your character write in their own voice – about their goals and struggle, about what motivates and worries them.

Was this letter written in a hurry? Are there tears on the page? Or blood? Is there a coded message contained in the words?

When you've finished writing, post the letter to yourself. You can send it through the mail, or – if you don't have a stamp – walk around the block and push it through your letterbox. Then, when you open and read the letter, it will feel like it's come from a real person not a character. And it will take your story in a whole new direction.

Have fun!

Yours sincerely,

ANDY

LET'S GET OUT OF HERE!

MAKING THE MOST OF LOCATIONS

Sometimes, a simple change of location can do wonders for your story, or a scene in your story. Let's look at an example:

Two brothers having an argument in their bedroom. Some shouting, a little name-calling, a slammed door maybe. This is good stuff, it's dramatic. But it's nothing unusual – we see arguments like this in all kinds of stories. So let's relocate it.

Why not have the argument on a roller coaster? The argument is freaking out the other passengers. Now, as well as the brothers, everyone is shouting and screaming. Maybe one of the brothers is so exasperated that he tries to get off the roller coaster. Way more dramatic than an argument at home, wouldn't you say?

Or we could set the scene in a supermarket, where we have the added embarrassment of other people watching. There are packets of cornflakes (or tins of beans) to throw. A stranger might get involved – perhaps the store manager or a security guard.

Which is your favourite? The roller coaster or the supermarket?

I'll bet it's not the bedroom. Am I right?

Likewise, think about where your overall story is set. Is the village where you live the best location? After all, you have the whole world, the entire universe, the long-ago past and undiscovered future available to you. Writing can take you anywhere, so pack your pencil and go explore!

FOUR INCONVENIENT PLACES TO HAVE AN ARGUMENT

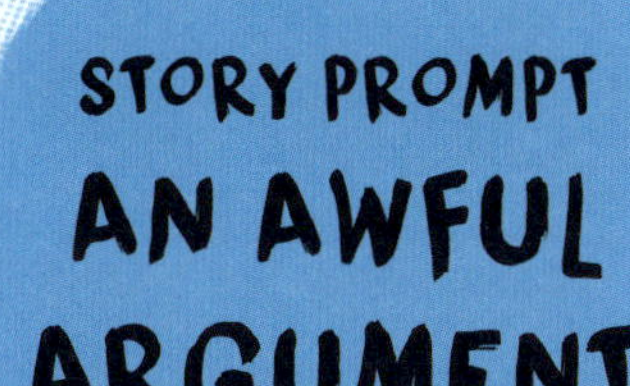

STORY PROMPT
AN AWFUL ARGUMENT

In the last section we discussed how much fun it would be to stage an argument on a roller coaster or in a supermarket. I think it would be a shame not to write at least one of them, don't you? So pick your favourite and let's write that ruckus.

It can be between two siblings, or friends, a married couple or total strangers. What are they arguing about? Maybe the setting can give us some clues? What would cause an argument in a supermarket? Or on a fairground ride? And wherever this happens, be sure to make sure to make full use of the setting.

Right, enough from me, it's time to cause some trouble.

PROJECT

THE WHEEL OF DRAMA

If your writing surprises you, then there's a good chance it will surprise your readers too. But how do we surprise ourselves? One way is to create … the Wheel of Drama!

Similar to the kind of device you might see in a TV game show, the Wheel of Drama is divided into sections, on which are written different plot points and obstacles such as: a hidden clue; a spy; mistaken identity; a character breaks the law; a lie; and gossip. Then you spin the wheel, see where it stops and find a way to work that event into your story.

Why not build your own Wheel of Drama! Use the ideas above, if you like, but you will also need to come up with new plot ideas all of your own. Aim for twelve ideas, but feel free to use more or fewer – this is your wheel, after all.

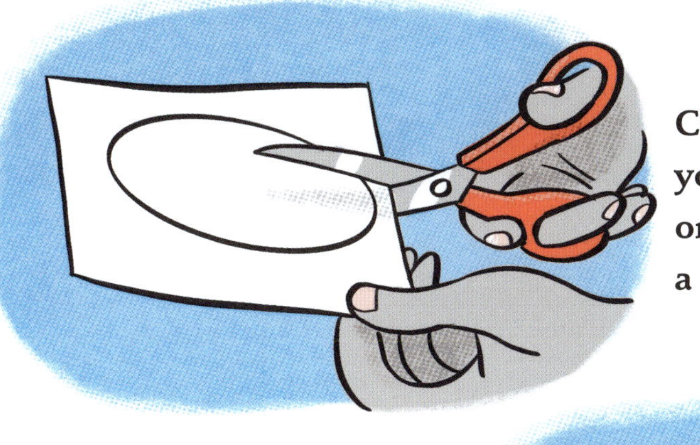

Cut a circle out of card – you can use a plate, pot or pan to help you draw a perfect circle.

Measure the diameter of the circle to find the centre and draw lines running through the middle to create your twelve sections.

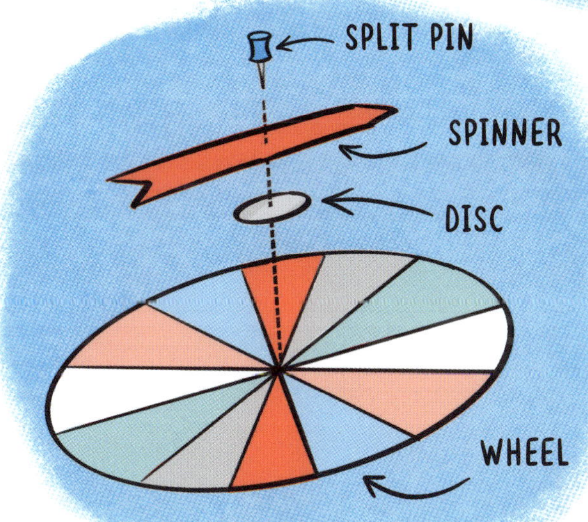

To make your spinner: take a piece of cardboard and cut out an arrow shape and a small disc to go underneath it.

Pin the spinner and disc together in the centre, but not too tightly so that the spinner spins freely.

Add the following plot ideas to the segments: a clue is discovered; mistaken identity; a character breaks the law; a lie is told; a stranger comes calling; a thunderstorm; someone has an accident; a mysterious parcel arrives; a pet escapes; something explodes; a bag full of money; a surprise party.

Now, just in case you were thinking no serious writer would ever build such a contraption, I'd like to reassure you that they already have.

Edgar Wallace and Erle Stanley Gardner – both writers of detective stories – used what they called plot wheels to spice up their stories. Mr Gardner, in fact, used several; for example, the wheel of complicating circumstances and the wheel of solutions.

Maybe you could make a wheel of obstacles. A wheel of weather. A wheel of character, a wheel of baddies or a wheel of opportunity. My favourite wheel is a big wheel of cheese – it doesn't help me write, but it's absolutely delicious with grapes and crackers.

THUNDER AND LIGHTNING

DON'T FORGET THE WEATHER

Elmore Leonard was a brilliant and prolific* author who wrote ten well-known and frequently quoted tips for writers. You should look them up, but don't take them too seriously – Mr Leonard was being deliberately tough when he compiled his list. Take, for example, his first tip:

> Never open a book with weather.

Good advice, but – as with all rules – this has been broken by many great and successful writers. The point Mr Leonard was making is this: get your story going quickly. Don't waste time describing unimportant details when you can get straight to the action.

*Meaning "productive" – he wrote many novels, short stories and scripts for movies.

What Mr Leonard doesn't say – but I'm saying here – is that the weather can be a very powerful tool for writers. We want our characters to struggle, right? Well, a change in the weather can cause all kinds of problems.

Think about an unexpected downpour, snow, ice, lightning! Think about sweltering heat, blinding sun and absolute dark. Strong winds and rumbling thunder. Felled trees, blocked roads, soaked clothes and ruined hair. Weather can wreck a well-laid plan, provide a distraction or a means of escape. And guess what? Weather happens in real life. So why shouldn't it happen in a story?

So if your story is stuck, or things are going a little too well for your character, a change in the weather might be just the thing you need.

STORY PROMPT

START WITH THE WEATHER

Sometimes, you should do exactly what you're told. If you're stuck up a mountain in a snowstorm, for example, you should absolutely do what your guide tells you. Other times – like when you're writing stories – you can do whatever you please.

So let's break Elmore Leonard's rule and start a story with the weather. In fact, let's do it up a mountain, in a snowstorm. But here's the thing – when the guide tells our character not to head off on their own, our character (stubborn, impulsive, a little bit rebellious) does exactly that.

Does our character get lost? Do they fall? Become trapped? Bump into a yeti? Will they make it to the bottom in one piece? Do they learn a valuable lesson? All of this is entirely up to you. Wrap up warm and get writing.

HOW DOES IT SOUND?

READ YOUR WRITING OUT LOUD

Writing can be a disjointed process. Filled with gaps where we … pause and … think … and … consider the next scene. The next word. Maybe we stop writing in the middle of a sentence and … come back to it an hour or a day later.

When writing in this stop-start fashion, errors can creep in. Grammar and spelling mistakes, of course. But there will also be words we use too often or incorrectly, sentences that feel clumsy and entire paragraphs that make no sense.

These things are easy to miss when you're writing. And they're difficult to spot when you read your work back, precisely because it is *your* work – you know what's coming, so your mind kind of skips ahead and dances over the page.

The way to fix this – to read your work like someone reading it for the very first time – is to read it out loud.

It's amazing how this simple act will reveal all the places where your writing has lost its way. You will see where it's lost rhythm, where you have repeated yourself, where character names have got muddled up and where you have repeated yourself. You will find subtle slips and great big clangers. And then you can go back and fix them.

Right, I'd best go and read this paragraph out loud – I have a feeling are there a fix things I need to few.

STORY PROMPT

DID I SAY THAT OUT LOUD?

We all have an inner voice. It's the one that says – in the privacy of our minds – what we really think: *This lesson is boring*; *Mum's cooking is terrible*; *My teacher looks like a werewolf*; *I really need to fart*. Thank *goodness* that we keep that little, honest, occasionally rude voice locked up inside our skulls.

But what if a character could no longer contain their inner voice and all their private thoughts were suddenly out in the open. Let's write that story now.

Think about how this came to be, who it happened to, and what situation you can put them in for maximum drama and embarrassment.

And when you've written it ...
read it out loud.

BUM GLUE

A FIRM FIX FOR FIDGETY WRITERS

Those of you who have read *Unleash Your Creative Monster* (and if not, why not?) will be familiar with Bum Glue – an essential piece of equipment that helps fidgety writers stay sitting on their chairs and – ideally – writing. To those of you who are new to Bum Glue – don't panic. It's metaphorical glue, meaning it won't mess up your clothes. But it does work. In *Unleash*, we gave readers three varieties of Bum Glue and it was so much fun we've come up with three more. Experiment with them and see which works best for you.

BUM GLUE #4

DESTROY YOUR EXCUSES

There are many excuses to avoid writing – *It's too hard, I'm no good, I'm too tired, I'm not inspired.*

Now, you can listen to these excuses, or – if you want to train your Creative Monster and write great stories – you can destroy them. And it's very easy to do.

Take a scrap of paper – any rubbishy, dirty old piece will do – and write your excuse on it. Now take that piece of paper – that rotten excuse – screw it up into a ball and dump it in the bin.

Feel better?

I knew you would. Now go and write something.

BUM GLUE #5
A FORFEIT

This is the exact opposite of a reward. Think of a job you would rather not do. Like washing your parents' car, cleaning the windows, vacuuming, picking up leaves in the garden, taking out the bins or tidying your room. Got it? Now go and promise someone that you will do exactly that, *unless* you manage to sit down and write for half an hour without interruptions. The choice is yours: write something or do something useful for somebody else.

By the way, you really should clean your room. It's a disgrace!

BUM GLUE #6

BEFORE THE NEXT THING

I want you to sit down to write exactly thirty-five minutes before something else starts.

Maybe there is an important football match on TV at 16.45. You sit down to write at 16.10 sharp. And you stop at 16.40 on the dot. Giving you five minutes to settle down for the footy.

Perhaps you have to leave for a family outing at 12.30. You sit down to write at 11.55. You stop at 12.25 then hurry up, pull on your coat and shoes and get out of the door.

Need to leave for a birthday party at 14.00? Start writing at 13.25.

Knowing there is a hard stop – a point at which you have to do something else – can make it easier to sit down and put in some solid writing time at your desk.

Having supper with the King at 18.00 – you know what to do. And don't forget to wash your hands.

STORY PROMPT

THE SOUP MONSTER

While writing Bum Glue #5, I had an idea for a story prompt: the child with the messiest room in the world. Let's call him Archie, and his room is *horrendous*. As well as the toys, books, paints, games, bags, boxes, socks and underpants, there are apple cores, mugs of sour milk and stale pieces of toast everywhere.

And then this happens: a discarded battery falls into an old bowl of mouldy soup. The soup bubbles, it fizzes and something – a tentacle perhaps – reaches out from the broth. Archie (or Archie's room) has created life! It might be good or it could be evil – it's up to you.

One more thing – Archie is trapped in the room with this thing. And (on account of his room being such a mess) he can't get out. He's trapped, with only the mess in his room to help him. Luckily, there's a lot of it.

IN
SEARCH
OF
MAGIC

SOME IDEAS ABOUT IDEAS

Inspiration is a mysterious and magical thing. If you could bottle inspiration, it would sell for millions of pounds. But, alas, we cannot.*

However, we can create an environment where inspiration can shine, magic can happen and ideas can grow. We do this by reading widely, by being curious about the world around us, by stepping into the next section and reading some of my thoughts on inspiration: my ideas about ideas.

*But you could write a book about writing and sell it for around £9.99.

ONCE UPON A WHATNOT

INSPIRATION FROM HISTORY

Let me start by telling you a historical fact. Wait, stay right where you are! It's interesting, I promise. It's about the window tax. Tax is money that people pay to the government to help pay for things like hospitals, schools and roads.

In the eighteenth and nineteenth centuries, the government thought it would be a good idea to tax people based on how many windows they had. The thinking went: people with more money should pay more tax, people with more money have bigger houses, and bigger houses have more windows.

But people hate paying tax* and are very good at finding ways to avoid it. Can you guess what people did to avoid the window tax?

They bricked up their windows. Look around, some of them are still bricked up today – you're particularly likely to see this in big cities and on old buildings.

*Want to see something funny? Watch your parents' faces when you ask them about taxes.

OK, history lesson is over. Now, imagine you are a young boy or girl, living in England in 1856. You wake up one morning and throw open your curtains, but the room remains as dark as the inside of a miser's pocket. Weird, because you can hear people moving about downstairs, you can smell breakfast cooking and you just *know* it's morning. So you light a candle. And what do you discover? Someone has bricked up your window.

Sounds like the start of a pretty good story, don't you think? Well, history is *crammed* full of story inspiration just like this.

How about the Great Fire of London, or the Great Plague? What about Mary Anning collecting fossils on the beach in Lyme Regis? The first man on the moon? The first woman to fly across the Atlantic? Imagine a time before the telephone, or just after the discovery of electricity. There are millions of stories out there, buried in history. All you have to do – like Mary Anning – is dig.

FOUR INTERESTING MOMENTS FROM HISTORY

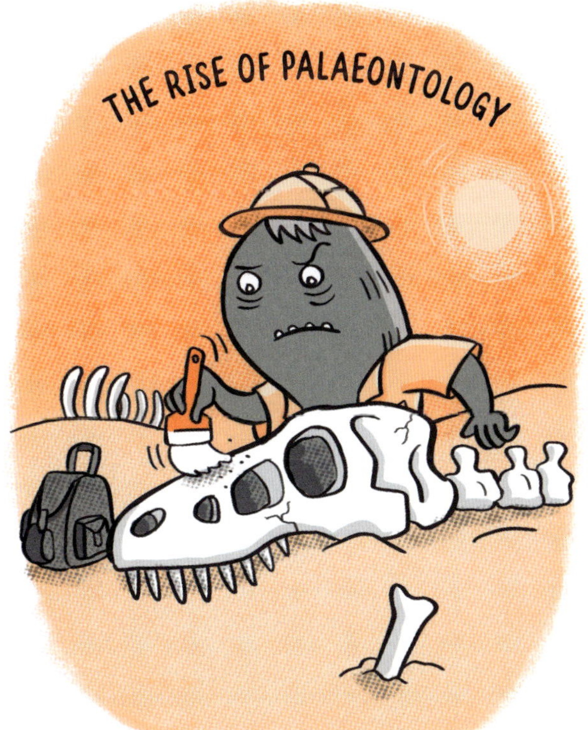

PROJECT

A FILE FULL OF HINSPIRATION

Why not create a file full of historical inspiration? Maybe you can collect all your ideas into a dedicated notebook or folder. Oh, I've just thought of a portmanteau* – you could call this your "Hinspiration File". And while you're at it, you can decorate the cover.

I've already given you some ideas on the previous page, but maybe there is something else from history that interests you. Ancient Egypt, World War II, the Romans, Maya, Victorians, Celts, Vikings or Suffragettes.

Make a note of these in your Hinspiration File and write down any interesting details, facts or names. Maybe you can print out some pictures and stick them in your file too.

*If you haven't read the section on portmanteaus (see pages 42–44), you might want to read that next.

Or type the words "unusual historical facts" into a search engine and you will find all kinds of weird stuff: that false teeth were once made from wood, Napoleon was attacked by bunnies and before we sent man to the moon we sent a dog into space.

Anything that makes you smile or makes you think – stick it in the file. The great thing about doing this – apart from it being fun, obviously – is that it is guaranteed to lead to some fantastic story ideas. Some of these stories will come to you in a flash. Others might need to sit for a while, buried in your folder like a fossil, a mummy or a seed – waiting to germinate and grow.

TOUGH STUFF

WHEN LIFE TURNS TRICKY, TURN IT INTO STORY

Life can be tough. Friendships break up, pets go missing, accidents and illness happen. Jobs are lost, marriages end, and your favourite pencil will one day run out.

The brave writer doesn't shy away from the tough stuff. She understands that it happens every day, to people all over the world. And because of this, the tough stuff can form the basis of powerful and moving stories.

By reading about the ways in which fictional characters deal with tragedy, we learn how to face tragedy ourselves. We realize that when life kicks us in the butt, we are not alone. Writing tough-stuff stories can be difficult, but it is also immensely rewarding.

So sharpen that favourite pencil and put it to use – give it a good life, writing great stories. Stories about silly stuff, crazy stuff, magical stuff, happy stuff and – be brave – the tough stuff too.

BAD DAY, GREAT STORY

We're going to write a story about something tough – a bad day, bad news, a break-up, maybe even a death. But before you start writing, I want you to think about the ending.

You might be tempted to search for a happy ending – where the illness is cured, the friendship saved, the pet returned. But I encourage you to avoid that for this exercise.

That doesn't mean your ending can't be uplifting, rewarding or even hopeful. Your characters can learn lessons and grow, they can make new friends, resolve to try again and inspire those around them. These kinds of ending are often the most satisfying of all.

PROJECT

ADAPT A PICTURE BOOK INTO A PLAY

A couple of years ago, my daughters and I chose a picture book* from their shelves – *I Want My Hat Back* by Jon Klassen – and turned it into a play. We made simple costumes, found props to help us tell the story, then performed the play in the garden. We only had an audience of three, but they're loud clappers, so it was a huge success.

We chose *I Want My Hat Back* for several reasons:

- It's awesome.
- It has lots of dialogue.
- And not many "inner thoughts".

Dialogue works well in plays. But thoughts can be hard to show on stage. You could use voice-over to tell us what a character is thinking, but too much can slow your play down and make it feel like an audiobook rather than a play.

*You can adapt any book you like, of course, but picture books have the benefit of being shorter, which is really helpful when you are putting a play together.

So see if you can find some way of "showing" these thoughts. Maybe in action – a character stamping their feet because they are angry. Or in dialogue: your character voicing their thoughts to someone else. You may need to invent a new character to help with this, but that is perfectly fine when you are adapting something.

You don't have to reproduce the book page by page, keeping every character and every line. The challenge is to find a new way of telling the story. So feel free to reimagine, reinterpret and make the story yours.

Maybe, if you're really brave, you can perform the play for your family or your friends.

A PEEK INSIDE OLAF'S HEAD

FOUR VISUAL WHAT IFS

In *Unleash Your Creative Monster* we discussed the power of two little words:

What if?

With a little imagination, we can turn these two words into exciting story prompts.

In the last book we had *loads* of what ifs like: What if a policeman was secretly a robber? What if I had a pet unicorn? What if a magician lost his powers? And so on.

Well, for this book we're going to do something slightly different. Olaf has drawn four fantastical, funny and inspiring pictures. And for each one, I want you to write your own what if.

Look at Olaf's pictures and ask yourself what's happening, how did it happen and why. Ask yourself who the characters are and what they are doing. Ask where this happens, when and what happens next. Then ask yourself, "What if?"

After that, I want you to write a story based on one – or all – of your what ifs.

OK, enough from me and over to Olaf.

OFF THE SHELF

RAIDING THE BOOKSHELVES FOR IDEAS

A great place to find inspiration is on your parents' bookshelves. Or anyone else's bookshelves for that matter.

Some of these books might be too grown up for you to read (and if you do want to read any, ask an adult first), but all we need for inspiration are the titles. Here is a selection from the bookshelves in my office:

1. *The Buried Giant* by Kazuo Ishiguro

2. *Cloud Atlas* by David Mitchell

3. *The Night Circus* by Erin Morgenstern

4. *The Haunting of Hill House* by Shirley Jackson

5. *Do Androids Dream of Electric Sheep?* by Philip K. Dick

Aren't they wonderful titles? They raise so many questions: Who buried the giant and why? Do robots have inner lives? And what is haunting Hill House?

You can also combine titles to make completely new ones of your own. How about:

One more thing on this. When I'm struggling to find names for my characters, the first place I look is on my bookshelves – at the Kazuos, Mitchells and Morgensterns, all lined up and waiting for a role in one of my stories. By the way, if you want to name any of your characters after me – you're welcome.

MASSIVE WOMEN

THE SELFIE OF DORIAN GRAY

EXERCISE

OFF THE SHELF

Choose a title from the five listed on page 156, or go and find one on someone else's bookshelf. Or how about jumbling up two or three of those titles to create one of your own? And once you've done that, sit yourself down and write a story based on the title or titles you chose. It's as simple as that.

THE LION, THE WITCH AND THE SHOE BOX

ALICE'S ADVENTURES IN SUNDERLAND

PROJECT

THE BOX OF ONE HUNDRED THOUSAND STORIES

I know this is a book about writing, but this next idea uses maths to help us generate a HUGE number of stories. We'll be using a story box to tap into the power of combinations, but it will be painless, and you won't have to do any sums, I promise.

STEP 1:

Find an old shoe box.

Cut three strips of card so they fit inside. Make half cuts along the strips and slot together so you have six compartments.

STEP 2:

Label the six compartments:

1. Period and/or Place (where or when is our story set?)

2. Character (what/who is your character?)

3. Who is (what is the character's main personality trait?)

4. Wants (this is where we write some character goals)

5. So and Otherwise (why does your character want to achieve their goal, or what will happen if they don't?)

6. The End

Think of between four and eight options for each category. Write these on small pieces of paper, fold them up and put them in the correct compartments.

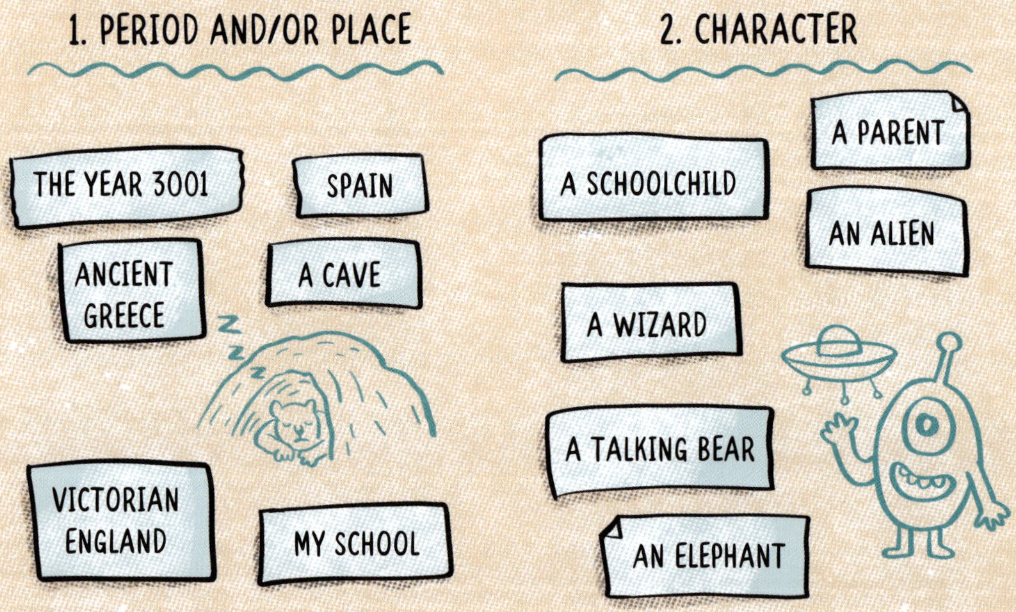

3. WHO IS
HAPPY
SILLY
EVIL
AMBITIOUS
TIMID
CHATTY
CURIOUS
MISCHIEVOUS
4. WANTS TO
SAVE THE WORLD
GAIN REVENGE
MAKE A FRIEND
BECOME A JEWEL THIEF
BECOME RICH
INVENT SOMETHING
EXPLORE THE WORLD
CAPTURE CRIMINALS
5. SO AND OTHERWISE
THEY CAN RETURN HOME
THEY CAN MEET THE KING
THEY CAN BUY A HELICOPTER
ZOMBIES WILL RISE UP
FAIRIES EXPLODE
THEY CAN BREAK AN EVIL CURSE
CHRISTMAS IS SAVED
AN ASTEROID STRIKES
6. THE END
HAPPY
SAD
BITTERSWEET (HAPPY & SAD)
CLIFFHANGER (ENDING IS UNCERTAIN)

STEP 3:

Close your eyes and pick one piece of paper from each box. Lay them out in order and you will have an idea for a story. For example:

At school, a chatty elephant wants to invent something; otherwise fairies explode.

If you put eight ideas in each of the first five boxes and four in the last, you get:

8 x 8 x 8 x 8 x 8 x 4 = 131,072 story ideas.

That ought to keep you busy for a while. Just remember:

1. You can draw more than one item from any box if you like.

2. If you don't like what the box gives you, pick again. You are the writer; the box is there to serve you. Not the other way around.

3. Be prepared for some absolutely bonkers story prompts.

FOUR FUN PLOTS TO FINISH WITH

Over the years, various people have tried to tell us there are only a certain number of stories.* They call them things like "the quest", "the vengeance plot", or "the coming of age story". Depending on who you listen to, the number of these so-called "master plots" ranges from a handful to a few dozen.

If you ask me how many types of stories there are, you will get one of two answers, depending on what mood I'm in on a particular day.

1) Two types – good and bad. Anything else is simply navel-gazing.**

2) An infinite number. Because everyone has at least one story to tell, and every one of us is unique. Also, anything else is simply navel-gazing.

*If you're curious, do some research into "master plots", "basic plots" and "dramatic situations". Not because you need to know, but because one of them might spark a great story idea.

**"Navel-gazing" is a phrase that means spending a great deal of time contemplating an issue of no importance. Why navels (belly buttons)? I have no idea, and I'm not about to spend the next hour contemplating the question.

Today I'm in an infinity kind of mood. But because infinity is big and this book only has 176 pages, I'm going to share with you four fun plots that I think you'll enjoy.

I've chosen them because they're all firmly grounded in character and (as discussed on page 81) story *is* character. See if you can build a story around one of these plots, or incorporate one into a story you are already working on.

Fish out of Water

Here, we take a character out of their normal environment, out of their comfort zone, and plunge them into a new situation or world. Importantly, the new situation must challenge and stress our character (just like a fish out of water, see?).

For example, an alien is stranded on Earth. A librarian is recruited to work as a spy. A boy from a posh school must adapt to life in a tough one. You can also reverse these situations: A human on an alien planet, a spy as a librarian, or a tough kid in a posh school.

Unlikely Buddies

This is similar to (and often combined with) the Fish Out of Water plot. In these stories, two people who would not normally be friends or colleagues are thrown together. They will have a goal to achieve and obstacles to overcome, but they will only succeed when they learn to respect and appreciate each other and work together. Examples include: A teacher and a student. A criminal and a police officer. A cat and a mouse.

Rags to Riches

I imagine you've already guessed what this involves. This plot takes someone from a state of poverty to one of great wealth. Maybe someone wins the lottery, finds a suitcase full of diamonds, becomes suddenly famous or invents something amazing. Typically, in this plot the newly wealthy character will begin behaving differently – and not always for the better. Perhaps they become spoilt or ditch their old friends. Resolution to the story comes when they learn the error of their ways. "Riches", by the way, doesn't have to mean money – your character may go from a little to a lot of something else, like friendship, opportunity or ideas. This plot also works the other way around – from Riches to Rags.

The Underdog

An underdog is a person (or dog, I suppose) who isn't expected to win or succeed. Maybe they are applying for a job, trying out for a team or entering a competition. But their chances of achieving this goal are poor – they are too small, too shy, too young, too inexperienced to succeed. However (and this is why we love these stories), it is not going to stop them trying. Who knows, they may succeed after all. And even if they don't, they will learn important lessons along the way and teach us – the readers – a thing or two about courage, dedication and determination.

One more thing: these plots often work well in combination. I've already given you one example – Unlikely Buddies and the Fish out of Water. But it's easy to see how a fish out of water could also be an underdog, or how an underdog might succeed when teamed up with an unlikely buddy. Maybe you can think of some other combinations of these plots?

PROMPTERCISE

LEARNING HOW TO FISH

This is the last prompt *and* the last exercise in the book, so I've combined them (and created a portmanteau) into a promptercise. Allow me to explain.

There's a saying you may have heard:

Give a man a fish and he'll eat for a day. Teach him how to fish and he'll eat for the rest of his life.

And so it is with stories – I won't always be here to give you prompts, so it's important you learn to catch your own and to feed your own Creative Monster.

So this last exercise is to write your own prompt, based on one of the four plots outlined in the last section. And then, of course, you are going to write a story based on your own prompt.

Writing your own prompt may seem daunting, but if you've got to the end of this book, then, trust me, you have all the tools you need (including the Box of One Hundred Thousand Stories or your Wheel of Drama!).

Just remember this – a prompt is not a full outline for a story. It doesn't contain all the answers. It's simply a challenge to yourself. And one that I know you will meet with intelligence, energy and creativity.

WE DID IT!

Wow. We've come a long way – you, me and your Creative Monster. And I want to thank you for taking this journey. I hope you've learned a thing or two. I hope you have created some wonderful characters and dropped them into a whole bunch of exciting stories. I hope – I really do – that you have been inspired. Because I know I have.

BELIEVE IN YOURSELF

(AND PUT YOUR BUTT IN THE CHAIR)

You've been at the front of my mind as I sat at my desk writing this book. And it has made me think very hard – and very carefully – about what to include. About what I know now, and about what I wish I had known when I was your age.

I wrote this book for you. But, in a funny kind of way, I also wrote it for me. For ten-year-old me.

Lots of readers have asked how old I was when I started writing books. I'll be doing a school visit or running a workshop and some youngster will put up their hand and ask the question. So I'll tell you now what I tell them.

I was forty. That's probably around four times as old as you are now. I've always loved reading, but I never believed I could become a writer. Some of it was not knowing where to start. Or how. Some of it – the bigger part – was a lack of confidence. *How could a boy like me possibly write a whole story?* Let alone an entire book.

Well guess what? I could and I did. It just took me a while to get acquainted with my Creative Monster. And here's the thing: if that little boy (me) can do it, so can you. So don't wait. Don't doubt yourself and don't put it off.

Instead, put your bum on your chair and your pen to the page. Trust the tips in the book to guide you, believe in yourself, your imagination and your Creative Monster.

I've really* enjoyed writing this book, and I hope you have enjoyed reading it as much as ten-year-old me would have done. If only I could travel back in time and show it to him. Actually, that's just given me a marvellous idea for a story...

*Totally necessary adverb.

AHHH YES, I REMEMBER ILLUSTRATING THAT BOOK NEARLY 3,000 YEARS AGO.
ANDY JONES
UNLEASH YOUR CREATIVE MONSTER
A CHILDREN'S GUIDE TO WRITING STORIES
AND THAT IS MY GREAT-GREAT-GREAT-GREAT-GREAT-GREAT-GREAT-GREAT GRANDFATHER ON THE FRONT COVER.

INDEX

IF YOU COULD SUM UP THIS BOOK IN ONE WORD, WHAT WOULD IT BE?
MAGIC!